COLLINS GEM GUIDES

MUSHROOMS & TOADSTOOLS

COLLINS
London and Glasgow

First published 1982

© illustrations John Wilkinson and
text Stefan Buczacki 1982

ISBN 0 00 458812 6

Colour reproduction by Adroit Photo-Litho Ltd, Birmingham

Filmset by Servis Filmsetting Ltd, Manchester

Printed and bound by Wm Collins Sons and Co Ltd, Glasgow

Reprint 10 9 8 7 6 5 4 3 2

Contents

How to use this book

Two great classes of fungi produce spore-bearing bodies, visible without a microscope: the Basidiomycetes and the Ascomycetes. Their arrangement into Orders and Families appears on the Contents page while the major differences between them are described in the next section. Several thousand different species can be found growing wild in Britain and Europe. This book describes and illustrates 232 species and it is hoped that it will enable someone with no previous experience to recognise most of the large and attractive or otherwise distinctive types that they are likely to find in gardens, fields, woods and parks. The easiest way to use this book to identify these is to flip through the pages until an illustration is found approximating to your specimen. A more sure way however is to use the simple Key on pp. 18–21.

With each illustration the species' scientific name is given, together with the English name for the relatively few types to have acquired one. Guidance is given on edibility and on the time of year each species appears, together with an indication of size; for each, the first dimensions refer to the approximate range in height and the second to the approximate range in cap diameter. For a few irregular types, only an approximate maximum diameter or width is given.

What are mushrooms and toadstools?

Mushrooms and toadstools are the reproductive structures of certain fungi and have fascinated mankind for centuries. The earliest, positively identified illustration of a mushroom appears on a fresco recovered from the ruins of Pompeii. Interestingly, it probably depicts an edible species, *Lactarius deliciosus,* and we know from their writings that the Romans were well familiar with the culinary value of such forms as *Amanita caesarea,* Caesar's Mushroom. Scientifically, there is no difference between a mushroom and a toadstool but it has become common practice to restrict the term mushroom to certain edible species. Moreover, the arrangement and classification of all fungi is still a matter of considerable dispute, even among experts. The system used in this book however is one that should be easy for inexperienced collectors to understand.

There is more to the diverse and remarkable fungi however than the structures we call mushrooms and toadstools and it is misleading to think of the group solely in these restricted terms. Other familiar examples include the moulds that grow on neglected food, while no gardener needs telling of black-spot on his roses, mildew on his daisies or scab on his apples, all afflictions brought about by other, less immediately apparent types of fungi. They are present in the air we breathe, in fresh and even salt water, and, especially abundantly, in the soil of gardens, fields and woods, from whence much of the subject matter of this book springs. Yet other fungi find roles as fermenters and composting agents, as sources of biochemical acids, flavours, vitamins, hormones and antibiotics.

Although studied traditionally by botanists, fungi differ from virtually all 'conventional' plants in their lack of the green colouring matter chlorophyll. As it is chlorophyll that makes possible the manufacture by green plants of basic foodstuffs from the raw materials of carbon dioxide and water, fungi clearly must obtain their nutrition from elsewhere and this they do by living in or on the organic matter of other organisms.

The important, basic structural unit of fungi is the hypha (plural hyphae); this is a microscopic tubular structure that ramifies through the medium on or in which the fungus grows and it is through such bodies that food substances are absorbed. Hyphae aggregate to form a mycelium and en masse give rise to the enormous range of structural form exhibited by fungi, including of course the mushrooms, toadstools and related reproductive structures that are our concern here.

The reproductive unit of fungi is the spore which is somewhat analagous to the seed in higher plants; it is the means by which individuals may multiply and disperse their offspring. Spores however are micro-

Some common types of toadstool spores

scopically small and are produced in astronomically large numbers. They are also very much simpler than seeds and do not contain an embryo. It is moreover the type of spore and the way in which they are produced that is the basis for the classification of fungi into their groups. The Basidiomycetes and Ascomycetes described here produce their spores (termed Basidiospores and Ascospores respectively) by sexual reproduction and it is these that are referred to throughout the book. Most fungi also produce other spores by a non-sexual process and the powdery covering that occurs on familiar mould growths is caused by spores of this type.

The Basidiomycetes, although numerically the smaller of the two great groups of fungi mentioned in the previous section, are the most important in the present context because they include all the familiar umbrella-shaped mushrooms and toadstools as well as the bracket-like fruiting bodies to be found on trees and fallen timber. Their spores are massed together on a special surface that normally takes one of two forms. Look on the underside of a cultivated mushroom and you will see one of these forms – many flat, plate-like gills arranged beneath the cap in

8

gills

pores

Ascomycete
cup

a radial pattern around the central stem. The dark powdery coating to the gills is caused by the spores themselves. The other common type of spore-bearing surface will be found underneath most of the common timber-inhabiting bracket fungi where, instead of gills, masses of tiny holes or pores are apparent. The spores line the tubes that lead inwards from the pores and drop downwards to be dispersed by the wind. Only one major family of fungi, the Boletaceae, combines the toadstool shape with the presence of pores, while two minor groups have folds or little spines instead.

The Ascomycetes, of which only a few are described in this book, bear their spores in enclosed, microscopic bag-like structures termed asci (singular ascus), and they are only released when the tips of the asci rupture. The asci are themselves formed within large fruiting bodies that are often either open and cup-shaped or are enclosed and flask-like with small holes opening to the exterior. These larger bodies correspond with the toadstools or brackets of Basidiomycetes.

Where can mushrooms and toadstools be found?

Although woodlands in general are usually thought of as the most important home of mushrooms and toadstools, one of the first things that the collector learns is that at least a few species can be found in most natural and even some quite artificial habitats. And the second thing that will be discovered is that whilst some species grow in a wide variety of habitats, yet others are much more restricted in their distribution and some indeed are confined to highly specialised ecological niches.

Realisation of this means not only that the likelihood of finding particular species will be enhanced if you know exactly where to look, but the chances of identifying a new find are improved by taking note of the substance on which it is growing and the vegetation that accompanies it.

The association of particular mushrooms and toadstools with particular habitats is not mere coincidence; it is a matter of nutrition. Species will grow where they can obtain their special food requirements, be this in the soil of acid heathlands, on the lawns of our gardens or among piles of rotting dung and compost. Nonetheless it is when we examine the reasons for the distribution of woodland fungi that the picture becomes even more fascinating, for the mycelium of many of these species does not merely ramify at random through the soil as does that of other mushrooms and toadstools. Additionally it forms a curious and intimate association with the fine rootlets of the trees beneath which the fungi grow. These fine roots become enveloped by a tangled mass of hyphae termed a mycorrhiza which acts as a sort of intermediary in helping the roots to take up nutrients from the soil. Such associations tend to be fairly specific, hence some species of fungi are always found beneath or very close to, certain types of tree – the Larch Bolete with larches and the Fly Agaric with birches for instance.

Fly Agaric
with birch

Larch Bolete
with larch

Mushrooms and toadstools as food and poison

It is a great pity that for many people, fungi as food begin and end with the cultivated mushrooms that they buy from the supermarket shelf or the reconstituted *Boletus* that provides the raw materials of canned mushroom soup. In general the people of Britain and north-west Europe are much more averse to collecting and eating wild species than are those of southern and eastern parts of the Continent. Indeed there are markets in Italy and Hungary for instance where dozens, if not hundreds, of different kinds can be purchased. There is no logical basis for the marked fungiphobia in Britain and the West and provided certain golden rules are followed wild mushrooms could become very much more popular. The first of these rules must be an ability to identify the handful of deadly species – the amanitas (pp. 38–49), *Inocybe patouillardii* (p. 129) and *Cortinarius* species (pp. 124–7), in particular. The second rule is to learn gradually to identify the good edible forms and to stick to eating only those that you have come to know well. In this book the edibility or otherwise of all species is indicated although there has been a tendency to err on the side of caution and indicate as inedible or suspicious any over which there is doubt or which can very easily be confused with harmful

An *Amanita*

An *Inocybe*

DEADLY POISONOUS

forms. Good groups to begin with are the various edible *Agaricus* species, the large lepiotas, most of the boletes, *Tricholoma gambosum*, *Flammulina velutipes*, puff balls, chanterelles, *Coprinus comatus*, morels and the fairy ring mushroom. To begin with, avoid in particular all amanitas and clitocybes, and all members of the Cortinariaceae.

Always collect mature but not over-ripe specimens, eat them promptly and never eat them raw. Wild fungi do not generally need washing nor should they be peeled; a few will benefit from having a tough stalk removed but otherwise they can be prepared much as cultivated mushrooms. So far, so good, but how can they be cooked? The short answer is that there are as many ways of preparing the different kinds of edible fungi as there are of most other foods. They can be fried, boiled, baked, stewed or added to sauces. The easiest way to start however, and probably the most popular way among mushroom gourmets in Britain, is to fry them in a little butter or bacon fat. A few species (the fairy ring mushroom and the chanterelle are the best of those mentioned above in this respect) can be strung up on a thread and dried for use in the winter when they will be very' welcome after they have been soaked to restore their original form, if not quite their original flavour.

However, some people have allergies or other adverse reactions to wild fungi that others can eat with impunity. For this reason therefore, it is very sensible to sample only one or two caps of species that are being eaten for the first time.

The poisonous fungi bring about their unfortunate effects in a considerable variety of ways and the consequences range from mild stomach upsets to serious damage to internal organs and even, in a very few cases, death, although the latter is almost always attributable to the one species *Amanita phalloides.* Even *Amanita* poisoning can sometimes be treated provided it is tackled sufficiently early. This can create difficulties as many fungus poisons do not begin to act until several hours after they have been eaten. If mushroom poisoning is suspected, however remotely therefore, it is imperative that medical aid is summoned immediately. It will also help greatly if some of the suspect specimens are still available and can be shown to the doctor. It makes good sense moreover not to eat mixed dishes containing several different species – not only is the initial chance of making a mistake greater in a mixed dish, but the likelihood of identifying any offending species later is greatly reduced.

Identification

The biggest problem in identifying mushrooms and toadstools is that, in most cases, you only have a few weeks each year in which to practise! This book is intended primarily as a field guide and, with experience, many of the species described should become recognisable on sight. No use is made in the key therefore of microscopic characters or of chemical tests. Nonetheless, only by collecting specimens and handling them will knowledge accumulate and the collector should become familiar with certain important features right from the start.

Collection and examination in the field

Collect only two specimens of each species; to take more is to be wasteful. Note if the fungi are growing attached to each other in tufts or clumps, are solitary (growing as odd, isolated individuals), or are trooping (groups of individual toadstools close together but not attached to each other). Then remove them carefully from the soil or wood on which they are growing, noting especially the form of the stem base and how deeply it is inserted into the ground. Note too the surrounding vegetation and other habitat details are and, while they are still fresh, any characteristic smell. Always carry your collection home in a rigid container (*not* a plastic bag) and examine them promptly before they shrivel or decay. You will find that half a dozen is the very most that you can cope with from a day's collecting.

Examination at home

Shape Although most mushrooms and toadstools are umbrella-shaped, fungi can range from bracket-like structures, through club-shaped and spherical objects to organs resembling cauliflowers, antlers or brains. However, all the non-umbrella forms described in this book are indicated at the beginning of the Key and it is with the many umbrella-shaped species that more careful attention is required.

Spore-bearing surface The four types of spore-bearing surface (gills, folds, pores or spines) to be found beneath an umbrella type of cap were referred to briefly on p. 8 and they are the first characters to be used in the key to the umbrella group.

Spore print colour The colour of the spores *en masse* is one of the most important features to be used in assigning the gill toadstools to their groups. To discover this colour, it is necessary to do more than merely look at the gills for this can be misleading. Whilst it is still fresh therefore, cut the cap from the stem of one of your specimens and place it with the gills facing downwards onto a sheet of white paper;

place an inverted jar over the top and leave it overnight. By next morning the spores will have been deposited as a white or coloured 'print' on to the paper.

Gill attachment If a gill toadstool is cut longitudinally, you can see the way that the gills abut onto the stem. This too is a valuable feature to use in identification and is also employed in the Key. The principal types of gill attachment are:

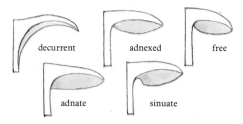

decurrent   adnexed   free

adnate   sinuate

Other features Many species have their own peculiar characteristics that you may need to re-check once you have reached a description but particularly important general features to look for are the colour of the cap, stem and gills together with the flesh texture and any colour changes in the flesh when it is broken. Note the presence or absence of a bag-like volva at the stem base, a ring part way up the stem or a veil joining the cap to the stem and stretched across the gills:

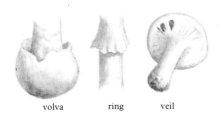

volva   ring   veil

Taste is especially important with some of the gill-bearing toadstools such as russulas. Collectors shouldn't be afraid therefore of taking a very small piece and chewing it on the tip of the tongue. Note if the sensation is hot, peppery, acrid, bitter or mild and then *spit it out again*.

The key

The key is very simple and in most cases does not attempt to lead you to individual species but to groups of essentially similar types – either Genera, Families or Orders. Having arrived at these groups, check through the relevant descriptions and illustrations to find your particular species.

The key presents a series of choices or decisions to make concerning your specimen. Each time you make a choice, the key will direct you either to a further set of choices or to the correct page in this book. The key should work with most of the large and obvious toadstools that you are likely to find but do remember that it *may* not work or *may* be misleading for small or less common species.

1. **Shape**

Skin-like, sometimes with curled-up edges, flattened on to wood or earth	Resupinate fungi, pp. 190–195
Bracket or shelf-like; growing on wood	See 2
Finger, horn, club or antler shaped	See 3
Cauliflower, honeycomb or brain-like	See 4
More or less spherical	See 5
Cup or bowl shaped	See 6
More or less umbrella shaped	See 7

2. Bearing pores on underside   Polypores pp. 196–211
   Bearing gills or folds on underside   Schizophyllaceae p. 174, Pleurotaceae p. 118 or *Crepidotus* p. 133

3. Finger or antler-like, rubbery, on wood   *Calocera* p. 214
   Finger or antler-like, not rubbery, on wood   *Xylaria* p. 234
   Finger-like or with complex, coral-like branching, on earth, brittle   Clavarioids pp. 180–183
   Finger or cigar-like, foul smelling   Phallales p. 216
   Small, club-headed, on earth   Geoglossaceae p. 232

4. Large or very large, stem-less, rooted to stumps   *Sparassis* p. 184
   Small, with stem, on ground   *Morchella, Gyromitra* etc. pp. 222–227
   Small, no stem, black, gelatinous, on wood   *Exidia* p. 213

5. Usually on ground, whitish to fawn   Lycoperdales and Sclerodermatales pp. 218–221
   On wood, tiny, gelatinous, yellowish   *Dacrymyces* p. 214
   On wood, tiny to medium, hard, variously coloured   Hypocreales/Sphaeriales p. 234–235

6. Irregularly ear-like, rubbery, on wood — Jelly Fungi p. 212–213
   Bowl-shaped, usually on ground — *Peziza* etc. pp. 222–231
   Tiny, bird's nest like, containing 'eggs' — Nidulariales p. 221

7. **Type of spore-bearing surface beneath the cap**
   Pores — Boletaceae pp. 22–35 (but also see pp. 210–211)
   Spines — Hydnaceae p. 186
   Folds — Cantharellaceae pp. 176–9
   Gills — See **8**

8. **Spore print colour**
   Black — Coprinaceae pp. 160–174
   Dark brown-purple — See **9**
   Pinkish — See **10**
   Pale to mid brown — See **11**
   White or creamy — See **13**

9. Gills decurrent — Gomphidiaceae p. 36
   Gills free, usually a ring present — Agaricaceae pp. 146–153
   Gills adnate or sinuate — Strophariaceae pp. 154–9

10. Gills free, toadstools growing on wood — Volvariaceae p. 120
    Gills more or less decurrent — *Lepista* p. 86 or *Clitopilus* p. 84
    Gills not free or decurrent — Entolomataceae p. 122

11. Gills decurrent, separating easily from the flesh; very stout toadstools — Paxillaceae p. 144
    Gills not decurrent — See **12**

12. Often a cobweb-like veil present between the cap edge and stem, esp. on young toadstools — Cortinariaceae pp. 124–141
    No cobweb-like veil; mainly fragile toadstools on dung and rich soil — Bolbitiaceae p. 142

13. Tiny toadstools growing on other, decaying toadstools — *Nyctalis* p. 89
    Toadstools not as above — See **14**

14. A volva or pronounced 'bulb' at the stem base	Amanitaceae pp. 38–49
No volva at the stem base	See **15**
15. A ring present on the stem	See **16**
No ring present on the stem	See **17**
16. Toadstools growing from wood or from buried roots	*Armillariella* p. 54 or *Oudemansiella* pp. 56–57
Toadstools not growing on wood	Lepiotaceae pp. 50–53
17. Gills waxy, toadstools often brightly coloured	Hygrophoraceae pp. 90–93
Gills not waxy	See **18**
18. Gills very widely spaced; medium sized toadstools growing in rings or tiny toadstools with hair-like stems	*Marasmius* pp. 77–79
Toadstools not as above	See **19**
19. Gills more or less decurrent, toadstools not growing in tufts	*Clitocybe* etc. pp. 66–69, *Laccaria* p. 70 or *Omphalina* p. 88
Gills sinuate	*Tricholoma* pp. 58–61, *Tricholomopsis* p. 62 or *Melanoleuca* p. 65
Gills sinuate or adnate; very small, fragile toadstools	*Mycena* pp. 80–83
Toadstools not as above	See **20**
20. Gills adnexed	*Flammulina* p. 76 or *Oudemansiella radicata* p. 57
Gills adnate or slightly decurrent; toadstools growing in tufts	*Lyophyllum* p. 64 or *Collybia confluens* p. 74
Gills adnate, toadstools not growing in tufts	See **21**
21. Stems tough	*Collybia* pp. 72–75
Stems brittle, toadstools exude milky juice when broken	*Lactarius* pp. 94–103
Stems brittle, no milky juice	*Russula* pp. 104–117

BOLETACEAE The boletes are mostly stout, imposing fungi, characterised by the presence in the cap of vertical tubes which open as pores on the undersides. The spores are borne in these tubes instead of on gills as in most toadstools. *Boletus* has olive-brown or rusty spores and differs from superficially similar related genera most importantly in the stem never bearing rough scales (unlike *Leccinum*) and in the cap not being very sticky in wet weather (unlike *Suillus*). The tube, pore and flesh colours and any changes in them when they are cut are important identifying features. Many species are good to eat although as they mature they are quite often attacked by fly maggots.

Boletus edulis (Cep, Penny-bun). This is probably the most widely eaten wild mushroom, a constituent of many mushroom soups and it makes an excellent dish, either freshly cooked or after drying. It can be found growing under most types of trees. The cap is usually smooth but slightly sticky when wet and can be of varying shades of brown although is probably most often chestnut. The tubes and small pores are white or dirty yellow, the flesh white and unchanging when cut. The upper part of the often bulging stem bears a white network. *B. aereus* is a very similar and closely related fungus, with a rough, darker cap; it is commoner on the Continent than in Britain and is said to be the most delicious of all *Boletus* species.
5–15 × 5–20cm. Autumn. Edible.

Boletus edulis
Cep

B. aereus

Boletus badius (Bay Bolete). *B. badius* is a species of pine woods. It has a similar cap to *B. edulis* but the dirty yellow tubes and larger pores and also the white flesh all turn blue-green when handled or cut. Moreover, while the stem may be faintly streaked, it has no network and is usually paler than the cap. 8–12 × 5–15cm. Autumn. Edible.

Boletus subtomentosus (Downy Bolete). A common species of broad-leaved and mixed woodland. The pale olive-brown cap quite often cracks to reveal the pale straw coloured flesh beneath (cf *B. chrysenteron* p. 26). The tubes and pores are lemon-yellow but soon take on an olive tint. When bruised, they turn, at most, only faintly blue. The fairly slender, pale brown stem is sometimes slightly ribbed. 3–8 × 5–12cm. Autumn. Edible.

Boletus piperatus (Peppery Bolete). This small *Boletus* is especially frequent under birch or pines. The cap is usually a shade of pale or ochreous brown, smooth and dry when mature although slightly sticky when young. The slender, similarly coloured stem tapers down to a characteristically bright yellow base. The large angular pores and the tubes are usually an intense rusty colour. The flesh is pale buff except at the stem base where it too is yellow. Most distinctive however is the often intense and unique peppery taste which makes the species undesirable for eating although it is not poisonous. 4–8 × 3–10cm. Autumn. Inedible.

Boletus badius
Bay Bolete

B. subtomentosus
Downy Bolete

B. piperatus
Peppery Bolete

25

**Boletus
chrysenteron**
Red-cracked
Bolete

Boletus chrysenteron (Red-cracked Bolete). This very common species usually occurs under broad-leaved trees. The soft, slightly velvety cap is variable but usually dull and greyish and its surface commonly cracks to reveal pink flesh immediately beneath; elsewhere, the flesh is creamy-yellow. The large angular pores and the tubes are also yellow, sometimes turning blue after handling. The stem is lemon-yellow at the top but reddish below and bears reddish granules. Although edible, it is often maggoty. 4–8 × 3–12cm. Autumn. Edible.

**Boletus
luridus**

Boletus luridus. This fungus occurs in broad-leaved woods (beech and oak especially) on limy soils. The cap, which is velvety at first, but becomes appreciably smoother as it ages, ranges through greenish browns to chestnut. The stem grades from orange-yellow at the top to red-purple at the extreme base and is covered with an orange-red network. The yellow-green tubes, and the small orange-red pores, like the stem and cap, turn blue-green or greyish after handling.

8–14 × 8–12cm. Autumn. Suspicious.

Leccinum differs from its close relative *Boletus* in having a markedly scaly stem and is also typified by the tubes and pores which are almost always white or off-white, and by the cap which is never persistently sticky. The various species (about fourteen are found in Britain) are not always easy to distinguish from each other but those illustrated are particularly common under birch and are shown as representatives of the two broad groups of brown-capped and orange-capped forms. Similar species occur associated with several other types of tree.

Leccinum scabrum, L. versipelle, (Birch Boletes).

L. scabrum is an impressive fungus and is consistently and very frequently found under birch trees. The cap is dull buff and the often tall stem white or greyish with masses of minute, rough black or dark brown scales arranged for the most part in parallel lines. The flesh is markedly soft, white and unchanging when cut. *L. versipelle* is another birch species, similarly robust but differing most notably in its handsome sienna coloured cap and in the flesh which discolours to pinkish when cut and eventually to dark blue-black or, at the stem base, to green. Both species make good and substantial eating.
L. scabrum 7–20 × 4–20cm. Autumn. Edible.
L. versipelle 8–15 × 5–20cm. Autumn. Edible.

Leccinum scabrum
Birch Bolete

L. versipelle
Birch Bolete

The genus *Suillus* includes those members of the family Boletaceae that have a persistently wet and slimy cap. The five species shown on this and the next two plates are by far the commonest of around ten species that are to be found in Britain.

Suillus bovinus, S. granulatus. Both of these handsome species are characteristic of coniferous woods, *S. bovinus* being especially associated with Scots pine. It has a buff or ochre cap with a very pronounced pale brown or almost white margin. The stem is similarly ochreous coloured and, especially when young, it has characteristic, tiny dots at the top. The tubes and the characteristically large angular pores, which have smaller pores within them, are also ochre but tend additionally to have an olive green tint and may darken slightly when they are cut. The flesh is usually off-white or sometimes faintly yellow in colour and may also be somewhat pinkish, especially in the stem. *S. granulatus* is usually a smaller fungus and tends to be more chestnut coloured with smaller pores. The flesh is almost always yellowish or straw-coloured and lacks any hint of pink. The special distinguishing feature of *S. granulatus* however is the presence of a pale liquid that oozes from the pores in damp weather and gradually hardens and darkens to a minute crust. If collected when young, *S. bovinus* is good to eat; *S. granulatus* perhaps less so.

S. bovinus 4–6 × 3–10cm. Autumn. Edible.
S. granulatus 3–8 × 2–8cm. Autumn. Edible.

Suillus bovinus

S. granulatus

Suillus luteus (Slippery Jack). This is a sufficiently distinctive species to have acquired a fairly widely used colloquial name. It is usually associated with Scots pines or other conifers and has a striking deep purple-brown cap borne on a pale buff but quickly darkening stem and, most obvious of all, a large white or off-white ring which also gradually darkens. The flesh is white, becoming yellow within the cap, while the tubes and pores are usually a dirty yellowish. 5–10 × 5–10cm. Autumn. Edible.

Suillus variegatus. Another species of coniferous woods but lacking a ring and distinguished by an ochre-brown cap with tiny brownish scales. The flesh is yellowish, and usually turns blue to some extent when it is cut. Apart from the scales and the generally less sticky cap, this species could easily be confused with *S. bovinus* (p. 30).
6–10 × 6–13cm. Autumn. Edible.

Suillus luteus
Slippery Jack

S. variegatus

33

Suillus grevillei (Larch Bolete). This species is often referred to as *the* larch fungus, for it is consistently and uniquely associated with the tree either when growing in plantations or as isolated individuals. The habitat alone should be adequate to identify it therefore, but it is also a very handsome and quite unmistakable species in its general appearance, having a very slimy, but lovely apricot-orange coloured cap and an orange-yellow stem which later tends to become more rust-coloured. The stem bears a yellow or whitish ring fairly near the top. The tubes and the small angular pores are also varying shades of orange-yellow but become somewhat rust-coloured when bruised. The flesh is pale yellow in the cap although slightly darker in the stem, whilst at the stem base it commonly turns blue after being cut. Although edible, most people who try this species find it to be relatively tasteless and its exceptional sliminess is also somewhat unappealing in this respect, although the slime itself is quite harmless. 5–7 × 3–10cm. Autumn. Edible.

Suillus grevillei
Larch Bolete

GOMPHIDIACEAE This family, unlike the Boletaceae, to which they are usually believed to be related, but like the remainder of the Agaricales described in this book, bear their spores on gills. They are sometimes known as spike-caps and are highly distinctive fungi, unlikely to be confused with any others especially when young and at their most 'spiky'. The cap is characteristically waxy and spinning-top-shaped and the spore print blackish or dark brown, but there is only one species that can be considered at all common.

Chroogomphus rutilus (Pine Spike-cap). A massive, solid-looking fungus found growing in coniferous woods of all types although it is most frequently found in company with various boletes under Scots or other species of pine. The cap is brown to brick-red in colour and is very markedly slimy when wet. It has a very pronounced and characteristic central point and bears dull olive or grey-black, widely spaced and decurrent gills beneath. These gills are covered by a partial veil when young. The often tall stem has ring-like marks near the apex and is usually more or less ochreous except at the base where it is more markedly yellow. Opinions vary about its edibility but it is not generally highly regarded. The only fungi that are at all likely to be confused with *C. rutilus* are members of the closely related genus *Gomphidius* but these are much less frequent.

6–12 × 3–15cm. Autumn. Edible.

Chroogomphus rutilus
Pine Spike-cap

AMANITACEAE A large and important family with only one common British genus, *Amanita*, characterised by a white spore print, and veils which almost always give rise to a volva and often to a ring also. The genus *Amanita* includes some of the most deadly poisonous fungi known and also one of the most exquisite of all edible species. A very few British amanitas (see p. 48) can be eaten but no inexperienced collector should ever eat any toadstool that has a volva.

Amanita phalloides (Death Cap). The most poisonous fungus of all; no-one unable to recognise it should contemplate collecting any fungi to eat. It has a wide range of habitats but is most common in oak or beech woods and is usually an olive green although varying from yellowish to white. The stem is commonly paler than the cap and has a large white, flopping bag-like volva and an almost skirt-like, regular white ring. The closely spaced, free gills are persistently white and never darken as do those of the edible mushroom. The flesh is also white except immediately beneath the cap surface where it may be yellowish. The first symptoms of poisoning (violent stomach pains, sickness and diarrhoea) may not occur until twelve or more hours after eating. Subsequently severe internal damage arises which may result in death although modern treatments can save many patients. Medical help must, however, be summoned *immediately* poisoning is suspected. 8–12 × 6–12cm. Autumn. **Deadly Poisonous.**

38

Amanita phalloides
Death Cap

Amanita excelsa

Amanita excelsa. This and the next species commonly retain veil fragments as flecks on the cap surface. *A. excelsa* is a summer fungus of mixed woodland with a very stout white stem, a poorly developed volva and a skirt-like ring bearing fine striations above. The cap is variable but most commonly dirty brown or greyish with grey flecks. The white gills are free or very slightly decurrent. Although said to be edible it is very easily confused with the dangerous *A. pantherina*.
8–15 × 6–14cm. Summer. Suspicious.

Amanita citrina
False Death Cap

Amanita citrina (False Death Cap). *A. citrina* is potentially dangerous in being easily confused with white and deadly poisonous species like *A. virosa*. It is however, more often yellowish and unlike the deadly white amanitas it has adnexed gills and a ridged, bulbous base to the stem instead of a bag-like volva. Its supposed smell of raw potatoes is said to be characteristic but this is so like the fresh, earthy smell of many toadstools that experience is needed before it can really be considered diagnostic. 5–10 × 6–9cm. Autumn. Inedible.

Amanita virosa (Destroying Angel). There is something decidedly eery about *Amanita virosa*, for its immaculate toadstools, pure white in their seeming innocence as they stand among the quiet of some lonely woodland, harbour a poison as deadly as that of the Death Cap. The name Destroying Angel sums up the strange and sinister aura that this species has, particularly in northern Europe where it is most common. Apart from its colour, the fungus is notable for its large, bag-like volva, its stem, which is often slightly curved and decidedly shaggy, and for its sweet and rather sickly smell; all characters that help to distinguish it from white forms of *Amanita citrina* which is shown on the preceding page. All the cautionary notes given on p.38 in relation to *A. phalloides* apply to *A. virosa* also and indeed its rather stronger superficial resemblance to the young stages of such *Agaricus* species as the Horse Mushroom, render it particularly dangerous. 8–12 × 6–12cm. Summer–Autumn. **Deadly Poisonous.**

DEADLY
POISONOUS

43

Amanita muscaria
Fly Agaric

Amanita muscaria (Fly Agaric). The best known fungus of all – the archetypal toadstool of countless childrens' books. It occurs typically with birch trees and although it is so well known, remember that large, old specimens may lose the white flecking and that the cap colour may fade. The familiar pictures of jolly little men in pointed hats using fly agarics as seats should not disguise the fact that it is highly dangerous.

10–22 × 10–22cm. Autumn. **Very Poisonous.**

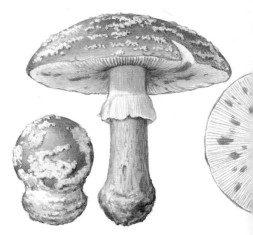

Amanita rubescens   The Blusher

Amanita rubescens (The Blusher). This species occurs with coniferous or broad-leaved trees and, true to its common name, always has some redness about it: the cap is red-brown with greyish flecks which may wash off; the white gills may acquire red specks as they age; the white, ringed stem is reddish below and the white flesh turns pinkish when cut. The stem base lacks a volva and is often mined by maggots whose tunnels too become red.
7–13 × 8–14cm. Autumn. Inedible.

Amanita caesarea (Caesar's Mushroom). Unfortunately this most beautiful fungus is not known from Britain but throughout much of Europe south of the Alps it is the most prized edible species of all and was well known to the Romans who, rather confusingly, referred to it as 'boletus'. Contrary to what is sometimes said, it is not confined to southern Europe however, and occurs sporadically in many countries. It occurs most frequently in acidic woods, usually of broadleaved trees and especially of oaks although in very few areas can it be considered abundantly common. The cap is yellow-orange with no flecks, the free gills are yellow and the ringed stem too is yellow although with a white bag-like volva at the base. It is a highly distinctive fungus with a combination of colour and form that render it rather unlikely to be confused with any other European species. It must be pointed out however that old specimens of the Fly Agaric (see preceding page) that have lost their flecks and faded, have been mistaken for it although they lack, of course, the highly distinctive volva. 6–15 × 8–20cm. Autumn. Edible.

Amanita caesarea
Caesar's Mushroom

Amanita fulva (Tawny Grisette), **A. vaginata** (Grisette). These two common and attractive species are the only British representatives of the genus *Amanita* that are both good to eat and at the same time sufficiently distinctive to render their confusion with poisonous types quite unlikely, especially for the more experienced collector. Nonetheless, the deadly *Amanita* species are so truly deadly that the cautionary note given on p. 38 about not eating any fungus with a volva until you have absolute confidence in your ability to identify them accurately, must apply to these two species also. Scientifically, however, the two woodland fungi shown on this plate are thought to have enough differences from other amanitas as sometimes to justify placing them in a separate genus, *Amanitopsis*. Both are to be found growing under broad-leaved trees, *A. fulva* being especially common under birch and *A. vaginata* under beech. The former is the more frequently found of the two species and is a clean, fresh looking fungus with an orange-brown cap that is very distinctly and characteristically striated at the margin. Occasionally a few white flecks occur on the cap also and at such times the fungus is most likely to be confused with its poisonous relatives. The cap retains for a long time its initial, compact, bell-like shape but it later opens out to become almost flat although still with a slight central bump.

A. fulva 7–15 × 4–9cm. Spring–Autumn. Edible.
A. vaginata 10–16 × 4–10cm. Summer–Autumn. Edible.

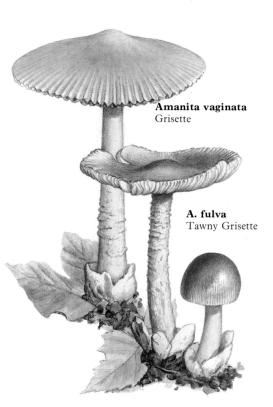

Amanita vaginata
Grisette

A. fulva
Tawny Grisette

49

LEPIOTACEAE A distinctive family of often large and beautiful fungi, superficially a little like the Amanitaceae in usually having a ringed stem with a bulbous base and with flecking on the cap, but lacking a volva. The spore print is white. Some of the larger species are quite delicious to eat but the group does include some poisonous forms also.

Lepiota procera (Parasol Mushroom).
L. rhacodes (Shaggy Parasol). These two immensely handsome species can be confused when young although *L. procera* subsequently becomes considerably larger and tends to be found most commonly on roadside verges and at the edges of woods where it may grow in large groups or rings. *L. rhacodes* is more shade-loving and seems especially frequent on rich soil in gardens. The caps of both fungi are brown at first but as they expand, the surface disrupts into brown scales on a whitish background; *L. rhacodes* is the paler of the two. The gills are white or creamy and the very tall brown stems have pronounced double white rings. The most useful identificatory features are the many dark brown bands on the stem of *L. procera* and which *L. rhacodes* lacks, and the flesh of the latter which changes from white to red-brown when cut. For many people, *L. procera* surpasses all others in its superb flavour: if the caps are fried in butter and served with a well-dressed salad the experience will be one to be cherished.

L. procera 15–40 × 10–30cm.   Summer–Autumn. Edible.

L. rhacodes 10–30 × 8–13cm. Autumn. Edible.

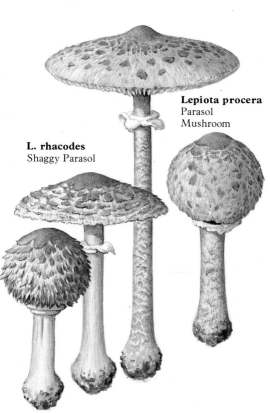

Lepiota procera
Parasol
Mushroom

L. rhacodes
Shaggy Parasol

Lepiota cristata
Stinking Parasol

Lepiota cristata (Stinking Parasol). This pretty
little fungus occurs among grass along path-sides
and at the edges of woods. It has a silvery white cap
with masses of small rusty brown flecks and a delicate
white or off-white stem with a small fragile white
ring. *L. cristata* has a characteristic odour when
broken, reminding some people of radishes and
others of tar, and which distinguishes it from other
small similarly coloured lepiotas.

4–6 × 2–7cm. Autumn. Suspicious.

**Cystoderma
amianthinum**

Cystoderma amianthinum. The genus *Cysto-derma* differs from *Lepiota* principally in not having free gills while *C. amianthinum*, the only species that can be considered common, is also unlike most lepiotas in occurring on heaths and poor acid wood-land. The cap is granular and yellowish while the gills are adnate and cream coloured and the stem bears ochreous granules below the narrow, flimsy, upward pointing ring.
3–5 × 3–5cm. Autumn. Inedible.

TRICHOLOMATACEAE A very large and important family of fungi that displays a very wide range of size and form although they are similar in detailed aspects of their structure. Although the spore print is usually creamy, white or pale pink, it is much easier for the inexperienced collector to learn to assign tricholomataceous toadstools to the fairly distinct individual genera than to the family as a whole. Within some of these genera however, specific identification may be difficult.

Armillariella mellea (Honey Fungus). A very variable and highly important fungus that is parasitic on almost all woody and a few non-woody plants bringing about decay and death of the roots and stem base. The appearance of clumps of ochre-brown toadstools at the base of garden trees and shrubs is an ominous sign and beneath the bark, and in the soil close by, black bootlace-like strands occur. These are the means by which the fungus spreads through the soil from plant to plant. The cap bears small dark brown flecks towards the centre while the paler stem has a pronounced thick white or yellowish ring. The gills are usually white at first but later become speckled with brown. Although rather bitter when raw, the young caps can be excellent fried but have never been as popular in Britain as on the Continent. Caution should be exercised when trying them for the first time however as some people are upset by them. 8–15 × 4–15cm. Autumn. Edible.

**Armillariella
mellea**
Honey Fungus

55

Oudemansiella mucida
Slimy Beech Tuft

Oudemansiella mucida (Slimy Beech Tuft). A readily recognisable white or greyish species to be found usually in large clumps on the living or, more commonly, the dead wood of beech trees, often quite high above the ground. The cap is markedly slimy with a somewhat waxy appearance which some people have likened to porcelain. The more or less adnate gills are widely spaced while the ringed stem is notably tough and fibrous. Although edible it is scarcely a very tempting fungus.

4–8 × 3–8cm. Autumn. Edible.

**Oudemansiella
radicata**
Rooting Shank

Oudemansiella radicata (Rooting Shank). This
fungus grows from buried roots of broad-leaved
trees. It is slightly slimy when wet with white, widely
spaced gills. The cap is wrinkled and yellowish
brown and the striated stem very pale brown and
often twisted with no ring but with a long, tough,
fibrous rooting portion in the soil. Like *O. mucida*
this species is only 'nominally' edible and not really
worth bothering with.
10–20 × 4–10cm. Summer–Autumn. Edible.

The large genus *Tricholoma* and its close relatives shown on these and succeeding pages have a number of distinctive features. The spore print is white, the stem fleshy and in all except *Lyophyllum*, the gills more or less sinuate. They nonetheless remain fungi difficult for the beginner to identify and it is not always easy to distinguish individual species.

Tricholoma   argyraceum,   T. pardinum, T. virgatum. *T. argyraceum* is predominantly a fungus of beech woods although it occurs in other types of woodland too. The cap is usually pale grey with a lilac tinge, the gills grey or off-white with yellow flecks when older and the stem predominantly white or pale lilac. It is edible but, like most tricholomas, unexciting. The non-British species, *T. pardinum* is an altogether different proposition however as it is very poisonous indeed. The cap is basically a brownish grey and is much larger than that of most tricholomas with a rough scaly surface and white or yellow gills beneath. It is typically a species of mountainous woodland. The distinguishing features of *T. virgatum* are its hot taste, its habitat under conifers, its pale brown or grey, lilac-tinged and markedly pointed cap and its white gills. Somewhat similar hot tasting species may be found under broad-leaved trees also.

T. argyraceum 3–7 × 5–8cm. Autumn. Edible.

T. pardinum   4–10 × 9–20cm.   Autumn.   **Very poisonous.**

T. virgatum 3–6 × 5–7cm. Autumn. Inedible.

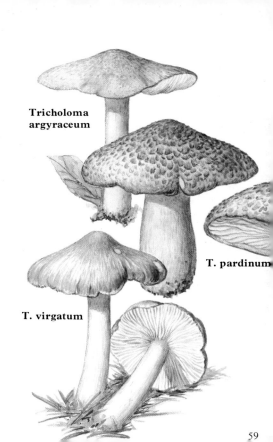

**Tricholoma
argyraceum**

T. pardinum

T. virgatum

Tricholoma gambosum
St George's Mushroom

Tricholoma gambosum (St George's Mushroom). *T. gambosum* is an exception to the general rule that tricholomas are not worth bothering to eat although its edibility is often overrated. It is particularly welcome nonetheless for it appears so early in the year; traditionally around 23 April, St George's Day. *T. gambosum* is a large fungus with an off-white or buff colouration throughout and is to be found growing among grass or under trees and hedges mainly on chalky soils; often in rings. The cap is smooth, the gills very dense and the smell characteristically floury.

5–8 × 6–15cm. Spring. Edible.

Tricholoma fulvum. A brown rancid smelling *Tricholoma* of poor, wet and acid soils, with a chestnut-brown cap having radial striations and flecked, dirty yellowish gills. The stem is also chestnut brown but markedly fibrous in appearance. 7–12 × 4–10cm. Autumn. Suspicious.

Tricholoma sulphureum. A small sulphur-yellow species differing from *T. flavovirens*, the other common yellow *Tricholoma*, in growing under oaks, or less commonly other broad-leaved trees. It is also characterised by a quite peculiar smell which is often said to resemble coal gas. 5–10 × 4–8cm. Autumn. Poisonous.

Tricholoma fulvum

T. sulphureum

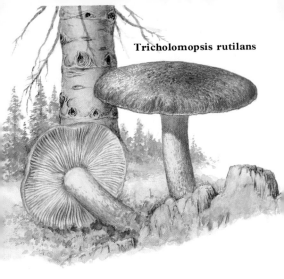

Tricholomopsis rutilans

Tricholomopsis rutilans. A large, very striking toadstool sometimes known as the Plums and Custard fungus on account of its very characteristic colouration. It has a deep reddish purple, powdery cap surface on a yellow ground colour and apricot yellow gills beneath. The stem is yellowish with a covering of powdery purple scales. *T. rutilans* occurs on and around stumps in coniferous woods and because of its dark surface it is often overlooked although its striking gill colour always causes surprise and delight when it is found and picked. 6–8 × 5–14cm. Autumn. Inedible.

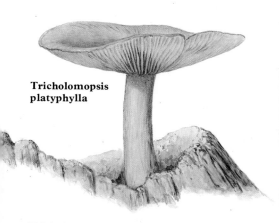

Tricholomopsis platyphylla

Tricholomopsis platyphylla *Tricholomopsis* differs from *Tricholoma* only in microscopic features and *T. platyphylla* differs little superficially from many brown tricholomas. The cap is markedly tough and pale grey-brown with fairly faint striations while the gills are white or pale brown and characteristically very broad. The stem is also white or brownish and fibrous and has a mass of conspicuous whitish threads at the base which serve to attach it to twigs or leaves buried in the soil. It occurs in deciduous woodland of all kinds throughout much of the year. 7–12 × 5–12cm. Spring–Autumn. Inedible.

**Lyophyllum
decastes**

Lyophyllum decastes. *Lyophyllum* differs from *Tricholoma* in its lack of sinuate gills but its most characteristic feature is its habit of growing in tufts or clumps. *L. decastes* occurs in woods and among grass and is also common on piles of rotting vegetation. It has a dirty yellow-brown, finely striated cap with white or yellowish gills and a usually curved white stem, brownish at the base.
8–10 × 5–12cm. Summer–Autumn. Edible.

Melanoleuca melaleuca

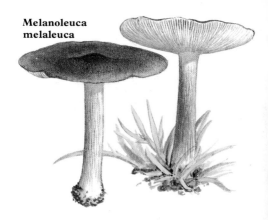

Melanoleuca melaleuca. Like *Tricholomopsis* and *Lyophyllum*, this is another genus of *Tricholoma*-like toadstools, of which *M. melaleuca* is probably the commonest and most distinctive species. It is to be found commonly in pastures and in woodlands of all types and although it tends to be somewhat variable in its colouration, it usually has a dark chocolate brown cap with pronounced white gills and a tall white stem with a brownish fibrous surface. The flesh is white and soft but has a tendency gradually to darken as it ages. A considerable number of other common fungi are often described under the generic name *Melanoleuca* but many of them may be merely variants of one species.

5–8 × 4–10cm. Autumn. Edible.

Hygrophoropsis aurantiaca
False
Chanterelle

Hygrophoropsis aurantiaca False Chanterelle. A delightful little fungus, best known for what it isn't, as this is the species that is most often confused with the desirable chanterelle (p. 176). It is, however, more likely to be found under conifers or in heathy places and is much thinner in texture; it is distinguished most importantly however by having true gills, not simple fleshy folds. It also lacks the chanterelle's apricot scent.

3–5 × 2–7cm. Autumn. Inedible.

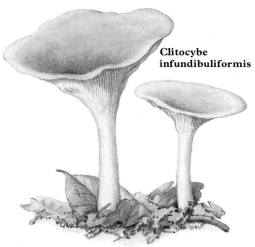

**Clitocybe
infundibuliformis**

Clitocybe infundibuliformis. *Clitocybe* and its allies are distinguished from most other white-spored toadstools in having decurrent gills and *C. infundibuliformis* is a typical funnel-shaped species, with a flesh-coloured, off-white or dirty brown cap and stem and whitish gills. The cap is markedly thin and the flesh white and conspicuously tough. It occurs in grassy places, in woods and on heathland.

3–8 × 3–6cm. Summer–Autumn. Edible.

Clitocybe odora

Clitocybe odora. A distinctive fungus with a predominant blue-green colour, thin white flesh and a strong aniseed smell which makes it a valuable flavouring although there are somewhat similar poisonous species. The gills are paler than the rest of the fruit body and less markedly decurrent than those of many clitocybes, while the cap may have a characteristically irregular margin. *C. odora* grows among grass or leaf litter, in woods and on road-side verges. 3–5 × 4–8cm. Autumn. Edible.

Clitocybe clavipes

Clitocybe clavipes. Another very individual *Clitocybe* species with a grey brown cap which is funnel-shaped at first but later flattens to give a form that has been likened to an inverted cone, cream or pale yellow gills and a most distinctive and fragile greyish stem with a highly bulbous base. The flesh too is white or greyish, soft and thin. *C. clavipes* is particularly common in beech woods but occurs also among other broad-leaved and coniferous trees. 4–6 × 4–6cm. Autumn. Inedible.

Clitocybe flaccida

Clitocybe flaccida. A rather handsome, fairly large, orange-brown fungus that is very commonly found growing in rings. It is sometimes confused with *C. infundibuliformis* (p. 67) which is usually smaller and paler. *C. flaccida* has the yellow or white, markedly decurrent gills and funnel-shaped cap that are so characteristic of the genus, and a pale ochre stem that often assumes a curved habit. The stem thickens towards the base which is appreciably woolly. The fungus is to be found in woods of all kinds but is perhaps most frequently encountered under conifers.

3–5 × 5–10cm. Autumn. Edible.

Laccaria laccata The Deceiver

L. amethystea Amethyst Deceiver

Laccaria laccata (The Deceiver), **L. amethystea** (Amethyst Deceiver). *L. laccata* is one of the commonest of British fungi and is found in many habitats including grassland, heaths and woods. It is variable in form and is not always easily distinguished from several other small, pinkish or red-brown species. Its most consistent features, however, are the widely spaced gills which have a powdery white covering of spores. *L. amethystea* is very like *L. laccata* in general form but is quite distinct in its violet colouration. *L. laccata* 5–10 × 2–5cm. Summer–Winter. Edible. *L. amethystea* 5–8 × 2–4cm. Autumn–Winter. Edible.

The most useful feature for recognising species of *Collybia* is the tough and fibrous stem, few other genera (except the closely related *Oudemansiella* p. 56) having the character to such a pronounced extent. They are known as tough shanks on account of this feature. Few of the species are edible.

Collybia dryophila
Russet Shank

Collybia dryophila (Russet Shank). A common fungus of oak, and to a lesser extent, other broad-leaved woods. The cap is flat and predominantly yellowish but more ochreous in the centre. The tough, thin stem which has a slightly swollen and hairy base, is similarly coloured or darker while the gills are white or yellow.
5–7 × 2–5cm. Spring–Autumn. Inedible.

Collybia
maculata

Collybia maculata. Tufts or rings of this easily recognisable species can be found in a wide variety of woods but are probably most frequent under pines or on heathland and seem particularly common growing beneath bracken. The stem and cap are predominantly white although they become increasingly covered with brown or red brown spots as they age. Sometimes specimens are found in which the stem continues into a root-like base. The cream coloured gills are markedly closely spaced and also tend to have red-brown spots while the flesh is especially tough and bitter tasting.

7–12 × 5–12cm. Summer–Autumn. Inedible.

Collybia peronata. This common toadstool is sometimes given the descriptive name of Wood Woolly-Foot, an allusion to the outstanding feature of the species – the pronounced hairiness at the base of the tapering white or yellowish stem. Leaf litter commonly binds to this woolly base when specimens are pulled up from the woodland floor. The cap is variable in colour and ranges through yellow-ochre to grey brown and is often marked with striations and darker streaks. The gills too vary from yellow to red-brown while the flesh has a strong burning taste. The whole fruit body is exceedingly tough and leathery. *C. peronata* is found most often under broad-leaved trees. 5–9 × 3–6cm. Autumn. Inedible.

Collybia confluens. This fungus is not dissimilar from the preceding species but lacks the woolly 'foot' and has only a downy texture to the pinkish stems which do however have the unusual characteristic of fusing together in leathery tufts. The cap is off-white to pallid and the fungus is found most usually in large groups or rings in beech woods. In addition to the four types of *Collybia* shown on this and the preceding plate, there are at least thirty other species of these tough toadstools to be found in Britain. Not all are common however and beginners often confuse them with species of the related genus *Marasmius*. This is not surprising since some fungi, including the two shown on this plate, were, at one time, placed in this genus.
7–10 × 2–4cm. Spring–Winter. Inedible.

**Collybia
peronata**

C. confluens

**Flammulina
velutipes**
Velvet Shank

Flammulina velutipes (Velvet Shank).
This is one of the few fungi to be found when
snow and frost are about. It is also extremely
common and grows, often in very large tufts,
on old trunks and branches of broad-leaved
trees. It has a lovely ochreous yellow and
rather slimy cap, slightly paler, widely spaced
gills and a darker, more or less velvety but
tough stem. It is an excellent edible species.
3–5 × 3–8cm. Winter. Edible.

Marasmius oreades (Fairy Ring Mushroom).
Many toadstools may grow in rings but none as commonly or characteristically as this pasture and grassland species. It has a bell-like, pale buff-coloured cap, tough, similarly coloured stem and very widely spaced gills. It is a very valuable species to collect, string up and dry for winter use but care must be taken to check that inedible *Clitocybe* species and others that sometimes occur in the rings are not collected too.

4–9 × 2–5cm. Spring–Autumn. Edible.

Marasmius oreades
Fairy Ring Mushroom

Marasmius androsaceus (Horsehair Toadstool),
M. rotula (Little Wheel Toadstool), **M. ramealis**
Three small species that often occur in large numbers on old twigs, conifer needles and leaf litter but are easily overlooked. *M. androsaceus* is probably the commonest and has a black, horsehair-like stem. It is often to be found among dead and dying heather stems. *M. rotula* has a creamy, unmistakably parachute-like cap with a thin, red-brown stem, whereas *M. ramealis* is slightly more substantial and less hairlike. It is especially common on old bramble stems. *M. androsaceus* 3–6 × 0.5–1.0cm; *M. rotula* and *M. ramealis* 2–5 × 0.5–1.0cm. All Spring-Winter. Inedible.

M. rotula ▷
Little Wheel
Toadstool

78

**Marasmius
androsaceus**
Horsehair
Toadstool

M. ramealis

79

**Mycena
galericulata**

Mycena is a very large genus of small white-spored fungi but the species are often difficult to distinguish.

Mycena galericulata. This species has a dirty grey-brown cap, a similarly coloured stem with a hairy base and white or dirty pinkish gills. It occurs, often in small clusters, on decaying wood and the stumps of broad-leaved trees,
5–12 × 2–7cm. All year. Inedible.

Mycena inclinata. This is a slightly smaller species than the preceding one and is common in dense tufts on oak stumps. It is brownish throughout, with the bases of the stems dark tawny brown and has a very distinctive rancid smell. The margin of the stem is striated and slightly irregular, giving it a toothed apopearance.

6–10 × 2–4cm. Autumn. Inedible.

Mycena inclinata

Mycena haematopus

Mycena haematopus. This species and *M. sanguinolenta* shown alongside are two of the *Mycena* species characterised by the production of red blood-like juice when the stems are cut. *M. haematopus* is the larger and less common of the two and has a predominantly greyish purple cap and stem (usually darker and reddish at the base); it grows in tufts on tree stumps.

5–8 × 1–3cm. Autumn. Inedible.

**Mycena
epipterygia**

Mycena epipterygia. A common species of coniferous or other acid woodland and also found on heaths. It has a markedly shiny yellow stem, a yellow-fawn cap and white gills and is noticeably slimy when moist. 4–7 × 1–2cm. Autumn. Inedible.

◁ **Mycena sanguinolenta.** A very common, solitary or trooping species found among leaves, pine needles or moss. Similar to *M. haematopus* in its 'bleeding' when cut, but smaller, more fragile and brownish in colour with dark-edged, white gills.
5–9cm × 0.5–1.5cm. Autumn. Inedible.

Clitopilus prunulus (The Miller). A highly distinctive member of the Tricholomataceae with pinkish spores. The white, sometimes flecked cap is often said to have a kid-glove texture. It usually has a markedly wavy margin and often a deep central depression so that it appears funnel-shaped and reveals its white or pinkish decurrent gills. The stem is white and often eccentric. *C. prunulus* usually occurs among grass in pastures but is found also on bare ground in woods, quite often in rings. It is an excellent edible species although it can be confused, especially when young, with poisonous white *Clitocybe* species and others.

2–6 × 4–10cm. Summer–Autumn. Edible.

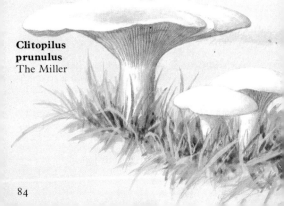

**Clitopilus
prunulus**
The Miller

Lepista nuda (Wood Blewit). The Wood Blewit is another pink spored, highly esteemed, edible species. The cap is somewhat variable in colour and although a rather beautiful blue-lilac when young, it later becomes decidedly reddish brown and often has a markedly wavy edge. The gills too tend to change from a rather intense lilac to a pinkish hue as they age. The stem is rather stocky, fibrous and blue-lilac. It is found in hedgerows and woodland and among compost in gardens and is sometimes confused with the true Blewit, *L. saevum* which is equally good to eat but which usually has a pale clay coloured cap and a whitish stem, flushed blue. *L. saevum* is also less likely to be found in gardens and is more typically a grassland species which quite often occurs in fairy rings. Both species have the useful characteristic among edible fungi however of commonly persisting quite late into the winter and in parts of Britain they can still be found for sale on market stalls. Some care should be exercised when eating either of the blewits for the first time however as a few people are known to be allergic to them.

5–10 × 7–10cm. Autumn–Winter. Edible.

Lepista nuda
Wood Blewit

**Omphalina
ericetorum**

Omphalina ericetorum. This small and very
pretty *Clitocybe*-like species is found on acid soils on
heaths and poor woodlands, often growing amongst
mosses. The colour of the somewhat funnel-shaped
and markedly striated cap is variable but most often
brown with white or creamy gills beneath. The
slender stem is pale buff and has a white woolly base.
2–3 × 1–2cm. Spring–Autumn. Inedible.

Nyctalis asterophora, Nyctalis parasitica.
These two very similar fungi will not be confused
with any others because of their habitats – on
decaying caps of other fungi: – in the case of
N. parasitica, these may be various species of *Lactarius* or *Russula* but in the case of *N. asterophora*,
Russula nigricans is almost invariably the host
species. The caps are dirty white or pale lilac and the
whitish gills are widely spaced or rudimentary.
When mature, they take on a dusty appearance.
N. asterophora, N. parasitica, both 2–5 × 1–3cm.
Summer–Winter. Inedible.

N. parasitica

Nyctalis asterophora

HYGROPHORACEAE This is one of the truly distinctive families of toadstools with some of the most brightly coloured of all species although not 'always easily distinguished from each other. They are sometimes aptly known as wax caps with their thick waxy gills and white spore print.

Hygrophorus conicus. This is a very attractive grassland species, although similar forms occur in woods. *H. conicus* has a yellow-orange cap, off-white or greyish gills and a yellowish stem, all parts characteristically turning black as they age, a feature shared with *H. nigrescens* (see next plate). 3–5 × 1–5cm. Summer–Autumn. Edible.

Hygrophorus psittacinus (Parrot Toadstool). Unmistakable, especially when young, for the dirty yellow, gradually darkening cap is then covered with green slime. This slime persists around the stem apex while the remainder turns yellowish. The gills too are a rather sickly yellow-green. Although occurring on lawns, this species will most often be found in pastures. 4–7 × 2–5cm. Summer–Autumn. Inedible.

Hygrophorus chrysaspis. This is among the larger species of *Hygrophorus*. It is distinctively pure white or creamy all over but gradually becomes spotted with brown as it ages. It occurs most frequently under beech trees, sometimes in very large numbers, although a similar species, *H. eburneus* is to be found under oaks. 4–10 × 3–10cm. Autumn. Inedible.

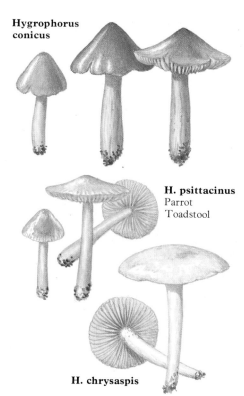

Hygrophorus conicus

H. psittacinus
Parrot
Toadstool

H. chrysaspis

Camarophyllus marzuolus

Camarophyllus marzuolus. Those *Hygrophorus*-like fungi with dry caps are now usually placed in the separate genus, *Camarophyllus* although this particular group of toadstools seem subject to more taxonomic chopping and changing than most. *C. marzuolus* is one such species although it does not occur in this country which is unfortunate for it is one of the few good edible spring fungi, and in many seasons it appears even earlier than the St George's Mushroom (p. 60). The cap is pale at first but soon turns almost black whereas the gills and stem remain whitish.

4–6 × 8–12cm. Spring. Edible.

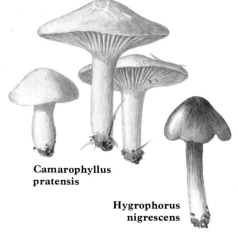

Camarophyllus pratensis

Hygrophorus nigrescens

Hygrophorus nigrescens. This species has a persistently white base to the stem. The cap colour ranges from yellow to red; the gills are white and the stem, although similarly coloured to the cap, very soon becomes black streaked.

5–7 × 1–5cm. Summer–Autumn. Inedible.

Camarophyllus pratensis. This is a very common grassland species with a buff cap and gills and a paler stem which often tapers downwards. The centre of the mature, flattened cap has a prominent central bump.

4–6 × 2–8cm. Autumn. Edible.

RUSSULACEAE A large family with two important genera, *Lactarius* and *Russula* which have white or creamy spore prints and characteristically brittle flesh. *Lactarius* species also exude a milky liquid when broken. Many are edible, few poisonous, but several unpleasant to eat. *Lactarius* species are duller but easier to identify than russulas although, for both, the taste is important (see p. 18).

Lactarius rufus. Probably the commonest of several pine wood species, having a red-brown cap, often with a central pimple, yellowish-buff but darkening gills, a red-brown stem and milk with a hot acrid taste that takes a minute or so to develop. 4–8 × 4–9cm. Summer–Autumn. Inedible.

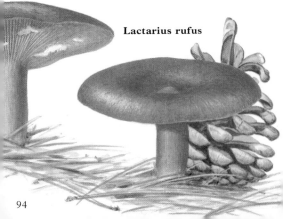

Lactarius rufus

Lactarius glyciosmus   **Lactarius vietus**

Lactarius glyciosmus, L. vietus. These two common, brownish grey or lilac species are found in woodland, especially under birches, *L. vietus* perhaps being found more usually in the damper areas. The gills are yellowish or lilac-coloured also and the stems similar but paler. The milk is mild at first but may soon taste slightly acrid. The two species are distinguished however by the characteristic smell of coconuts present in *L. glyciosmus* and by the milk which remains white with this species but turns grey in the air with *L. vietus*.

L. glyciosmus 2–5 × 2–7cm. Autumn. Edible.
L. vietus 4–8 × 3–8cm. Autumn. Inedible.

Lactarius vellereus

Lactarius piperatus, L. vellereus. *L. piperatus* is a fairly common. large white or slightly creamy species to be found in broad-leaved woods. The broad cap is often more or less funnel shaped while the taste, as may be guessed from its name, is instantly hot, peppery and acrid. A similar but quite often larger and even more conspicuous species with a more flattened cap and more widely spaced gills, is *L. vellereus*. When young this species has a markedly inrolled and velvety cap margin. The milk is acrid but less so than that of *L. piperatus*.

L. piperatus 3–7 × 5–20cm. Summer–Autumn. Inedible.

L. vellereus 5–10 × 10–25cm. Autumn. Inedible.

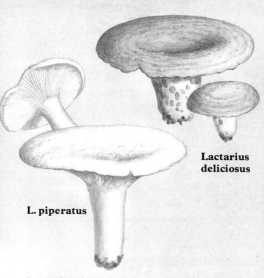

**Lactarius
deliciosus**

L. piperatus

Lactarius deliciosus. A lovely red-orange fungus with darker banding on the cap and orange-yellow gills to be found in coniferous woods, usually under pines. The stem commonly has greenish spots when old, while the milk is orange and mild or sometimes slightly bitter. It is a very good edible species but is now believed to encompass several closely related forms, some of which make better eating than others. 3–5 × 4–10cm. Summer–Autumn. Edible.

Lactarius tabidus. A species that is typically associated with damp birch woodland although it can also be found in other broad-leaved woods. The cap, which usually has a slight central pimple, is of a dull orange colour, the gills are yellow-brown, and the milk is white but turns yellow if a drop is touched onto a white handkerchief. The taste is very slightly acrid. 1–4 × 2–5cm. Autumn. Inedible.

Lactarius quietus (Oak Milk Cap). Probably the commonest British *Lactarius*. Its red-brown, faintly zoned cap and similarly coloured stem, pale brownish gills and white, mild or faintly bitter milk are not dissimilar from several other species. As its common name suggests however, *L. quietus* is distinguished by only being found in the vicinity of oak trees and also by a rather spongy stem and a somewhat oily smell that, when such things were common, people used to say reminded them of bugs!
4–8 × 3–8cm. Autumn. Inedible.

Lactarius turpis. Sometimes called the Ugly Milk Cap, this is a distinctive, large, olive-brown or almost black-capped fungus that, like many *Lactarius* species, occurs under birch trees but often among dense vegetation and is therefore easily overlooked. The gills are yellow-cream, the stem slimy and similar to, or slightly lighter than the cap. The milk is very hot and acrid. Although it is said to be edible after appropriate treatment such as boiling, it is better avoided.
3–8 × 6–20cm. Autumn. Inedible.

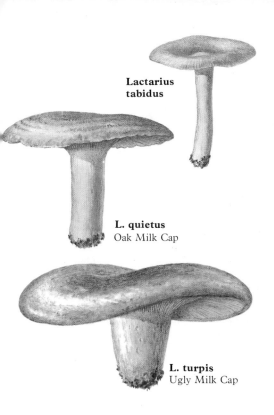

Lactarius tabidus

L. quietus
Oak Milk Cap

L. turpis
Ugly Milk Cap

Lactarius torminosus

Lactarius torminosus. This is, without doubt, the loveliest British *Lactarius* species. It is to be found especially on heaths and in poor acid woodlands, very often closely associated with birch trees. The cap is a pale salmon pink, concentrically zoned and with a central depression, an incurved margin and an overall rather shaggy appearance. The gills and stem are similarly coloured, the latter being gently downy. The milk is markedly hot and acrid and while this fungus has been considered edible in some areas, it is really one to look at rather than eat and may actually be poisonous.

4–9 × 5–12cm. Autumn. Suspicious.

Lactarius subdulcis

L. camphoratus

Lactarius subdulcis. Another red-brown species but with paler gills and with a general tendency to fade to a reddish buff as it ages. There is a mild taste, soon tending to turn slightly bitter, and copious, rather watery white milk. *L. subdulcis* is found in broad-leaved woods and is usually commonest under beech. 2–5 × 5–8cm. Autumn. Inedible.

Lactarius camphoratus. A distinctive fungus, to be found principally under conifers although it can occur also in broad-leaved woods. Whilst it is similar to a number of other species in its overall red-brown colour and mild, thin milk, it can be recognised by a curious spice-like smell that develops as it dries. 2–5 × 2–5cm. Autumn. Inedible.

Lactarius blennius

Lactarius blennius. There are not many greenish *Lactarius* species. *L. turpis* (p. 98) is a very common one; *L. blennius* is another but it is paler, somewhat blotchy and with considerably more brown and grey in its overall colouration. The darker blotches tend to be arranged rather regularly in concentric bands on the cap surface. The gills are very pale greyish, the milk is white but turns grey on drying and the taste is especially hot and acrid. Unlike *L. turpis*, *L. blennius* is most common in beech woods although it does occur in other broad-leaved woods too. 4–5 × 4–8cm. Autumn. Inedible.

Lactarius mitissimus. This is a very distinctive, rather vivid orange species, having a somewhat shiny, velvety cap with incurved margins, a slight central pimple and no concentric rings. The gills are considerably paler, while the milk is distinctly copious and mild tasting. *L. mitissimus* is a frequent species in woodland of all kinds although a number of related forms are superficially rather similar. Whilst some are edible, some are not and as this group of fungi is not always easy to identify, even for the experienced collector, it is safest not to experiment.

2–8 × 3–7cm. Autumn. Inedible.

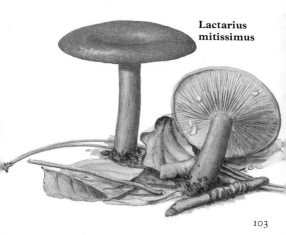

**Lactarius
mitissimus**

Russula is easily the most significant genus of large toadstools that the collector will encounter in Britain – there are well over one hundred different species to be found here. Like *Lactarius*, *Russula* species are not easy to identify although they have the merit of being generally brighter coloured and more attractive.

Russula claroflava (Yellow Swamp Russula).
R. ochroleuca (Common Yellow Russula). Two common yellow species, *R. ochroleuca* being one of the most frequent of all toadstools in all types of woodland whereas the very beautiful *R. claroflava* is confined to wet birch woods. Both have very appropriate names for *R. claroflava* has a bright chrome yellow cap and yellow gills, while *R. ochroleuca* has a more ochreous cap and creamy gills. Both have a mild or slightly burning taste but whereas *R. claroflava* is good to eat, *R. ochroleuca* is much less so and it is probably wisest to avoid it.
R. claroflava 4–10 × 4–10cm. Autumn. Edible.
R. ochroleuca 4–8 × 5–12cm. Autumn. Inedible.

Russula lutea (Small Yellow Russula). Another yellow species, usually smaller than most others and occurring under a wide range of broad-leaved trees. It is characterised by a mild taste, ripe smell of apricot and by the colour of the cap and gills which are rich yellow-orange and contrast markedly with the white stem.
2–6 × 2–7cm. Autumn. Edible.

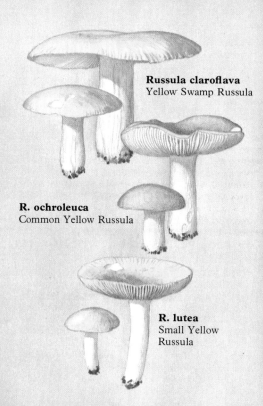

Russula claroflava
Yellow Swamp Russula

R. ochroleuca
Common Yellow Russula

R. lutea
Small Yellow
Russula

Russula fellea (Geranium-scented Russula). This very lovely and extremely common species is to be found in beech woods. It has a honey-tinted cap and slightly paler gills and stem. The taste is markedly bitter and very hot while, as its common name suggests, the whole fruit body has the scent of geraniums. Although it is sometimes said to be edible it should be left alone.

2–6 × 4–8cm. Autumn. Inedible.

Russula aeruginea (Grass-green Russula). This is probably the commonest of the consistently green-capped *Russula* species although some others may range through yellows to green. It tends, moreover, to be more grey-green than the clear colour of grass and is also sometimes marked with rust-red spots. The gills are creamy yellow, the stem white, the taste mild and there is little smell. *R. aeruginea* is usually associated with birch trees.

4–8 × 5–12cm. Autumn. Inedible.

Russula delica. A large white species found in woodland of all types and usually having a brownish hint to the cap surface which commonly becomes decidedly funnel-shaped with age. There is a distinct and decidedly unpleasant smell that is reminiscent of decaying flesh. The taste is acrid and usually strong and the flesh is characteristically hard. *R. delica* is superficially very like the large white *Lactarius* species, *L. piperatus* and *L. vellereus* but, of course, it lacks the milk that these fungi exude.

2–6 × 5–16cm. Autumn. Inedible.

Russula fellea
Geranium-scented Russula

R. aeruginea
Grass-green Russula

R. delica

**Russula
nigricans**
Blackening
Russula

Russula nigricans (Blackening Russula). This is a species of mixed woodland, with brownish gills, a dirty white stem and a whitish but rapidly browning then blackening cap. The gills are widely spaced, the taste is hot and there is a rich fruity smell. 3–8 × 5–18cm. Autumn. Inedible.

Russula densifolia. A dull brown or dirty white funnel-shaped cap, creamy, very crowded gills, a white stem and hard white flesh that turns red and later black when broken are the features of this species of broad-leaved and coniferous woods. The taste is variable, often mild at first but later becoming hotter. 3–6 × 5–15cm. Autumn. Inedible.

**Russula
densifolia**

R. sororia

Russula sororia. This species has a dirty brown cap, striated and warty at the edge, with off-white gills and stem and is usually found under oak trees. The taste is mild at first, then hot, and the smell is unpleasant – cheesy or oily.
3–6 × 3–6cm. Autumn. Inedible.

Russula foetens
Stinking Russula

Russula foetens (Stinking Russula). Rather like a large *Russula sororia* in general appearance having a slimy, dull honey-coloured cap with a knobbly margin, dirty cream gills and a white or off-white stem. It has a hot taste and a strange unpleasant, oily smell but, unlike *R. sororia*, can be found in all types of woodland and also in parks.
5–12 ×6–12cm. Autumn. **Poisonous.**

Russula emetica
The Sickener

R. mairei
Beech Sickener

Russula emetica (The Sickener), **R. mairei** (Beech Sickener). Two common red russulas (some other red species are shown on the next page) with creamy gills, white stems and a hot taste. *R. emetica* however has a rich scarlet colour and is found on wet acid soils, especially with pines while *R. mairei* is a beech wood species and usually paler red, sometimes with slightly greenish gills and a faint smell of coconut. *R. emetica* induces vomiting and should never be eaten.

R. emetica 5–8 × 5–10cm. Autumn. **Poisonous.**
R. mairei 2–4 × 3–6cm. Autumn. Inedible.

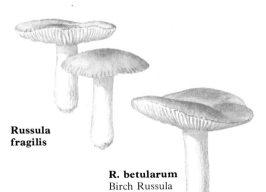

**Russula
fragilis**

R. betularum
Birch Russula

Russula fragilis. Some more reddish *Russula* species are shown on this and the next page. They differ in a number of important respects however. *R. fragilis* is, like *R. xerampelina* (opposite), a rather variable but smaller fungus and most commonly is pale pink-violet with white gills, a white stem, very hot taste and slightly fruity smell. It occurs in a wide variety of woodlands.
3–6 × 2–6cm. Autumn. Inedible.

Russula betularum (Birch Russula). As its name suggests, this is a birch wood species. It has a pale rose-pink cap, palest in the centre, and white gills and stem. It is very commonly confused with *R. emetica* (p. 111).
3–7 × 2–5cm. Autumn. Inedible.

**Russula
xerampelina**

Russula xerampelina. This is a remarkably
variable species, having a cap colour that ranges
through reds and purples to fawn and dark brown.
The gills are ochre coloured and the stem white or
pinkish but becoming pale brown when handled.
The taste is mild. It is common under broad-leaved
trees, especially beech and oak and has a distinctive
smell, somewhat reminiscent of fish or crabs.
Although *R. xerampelina* is edible, there are so many
unpleasant reddish russulas that are easily confused
that it is sensible not to eat any of them.
3–10 × 5–15cm. Autumn. Edible.

**Russula
cyanoxantha**

Russula cyanoxantha. This is a very common species to be found in broad-leaved woods, in parkland and even, on occasion, in pastures. The cap is consistently dark-coloured, usually olive green or brown but often with hints of deep purple also. The gills and stem are white and the taste is mild. Although many russulas are known descriptively as 'brittle gills', this species is an exception to the general rule for the gills are quite soft and pliable. 5–10 × 5–15cm. Summer-Autumn. Inedible.

**Russula
lepida**

R. vesca
Bared Teeth Russula

Russula lepida. Yet another red species, common under beech and oak trees. The rose-pink cap usually has a characteristic whitish bloom while the gills are creamy and the stem white with a pinkish tinge. There is a sweetish smell and the taste is mild. 3–8 × 5–10cm. Autumn. Inedible.

Russula vesca (Bared Teeth Russula). A variable species of broad-leaved woods, especially of beech and oak; the cap colour ranging through pale red-purple to pale brown or olive. The gills are creamy, the stem white, the smell fruity and the flesh has a nutty taste. The cap skin seems too small and barely to reach the margin so that the gill edges appear jagged, like bared teeth.
3–10 × 5–10cm. Spring-Autumn. Edible.

Russula atropurpurea

Russula atropurpurea. A truly striking and distinctive species and one of the most readily recognisable of russulas, having a deep red-purple cap with a darker, almost black centre. The gills are creamy and the stem is white but becoming greyish as it ages. The taste varies; in some specimens it is persistently mild but in others can be quite hot. There is a slightly fruity smell. Although *R. atropurpurea* can occur in all types of woodland it is commonest under broad-leaved trees, especially oaks. 3–5 × 4–10cm. Autumn. Edible.

Russula parazurea

Russula parazurea. This is a fairly common species to be found in broad-leaved woodland of most types but is especially frequent under oak and beech trees. It has a curiously coloured cap; a blend of grey-blue, green, brown and a touch of violet. The gills are pale buff, the stem white and the taste mild. A somewhat similar but rather more bluish fungus can occasionally be found in coniferous woods and there are several other russulas of this type which may, perhaps, all belong to the same species. 3–8 × 3–8cm. Autumn. Inedible.

PLEUROTACEAE Although there are few common British representatives, the family Pleurotaceae includes one of the most popular of all the world's edible fungi, the shiitake mushroom which is cultivated and cherished in many parts of the Far East. Almost all members of the family are to be found growing on wood, often with eccentric or bracket-like fruit bodies and producing white or creamy spores.

Pleurotus ostreatus (Oyster Mushroom). It is rather unlikely that the oyster mushroom will be mistaken for any other although there are one or two closely related whitish species that can be confused with old, faded specimens. Its clusters of deep, bluish grey, shell or bracket-shaped fruit bodies will be found on the trunks of most types of broad-leaved trees, sometimes at a considerable height from the ground when their gills are readily apparent and cause surprise to the inexperienced collector who expects bracket-like fruit bodies always to have pores beneath. This is a very good edible species, especially when young, and there has been some success in cultivating it artificially for this purpose. 2–3 × 6–15cm. All year. Edible.

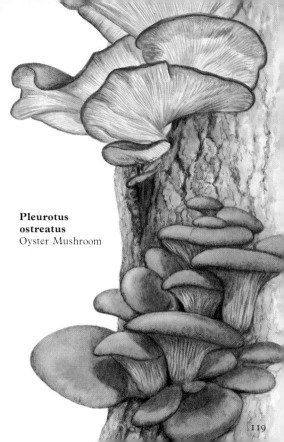

Pleurotus ostreatus
Oyster Mushroom

VOLVARIACEAE The only really important genus of the Volvariaceae in Europe is *Pluteus*, although in other, warmer parts of the world, the genus *Volvariella* (which does have a few British representatives), is more significant with a number of very good edible species. The Volvariaceae have free gills and a pink spore print and usually grow on decaying wood, woody debris or rich humus.

Pluteus cervinus (Fawn Pluteus). *Pluteus* is a large genus but *P. cervinus* is the only really common British species. It has a striated, bell-shaped, variable but usually dark brown cap that later flattens and is easily separated from the whitish, brown-streaked stem. The gills are free, white, becoming pinkish and the fungus is found in woods of all types, growing on fallen logs and also piles of woody debris such as chippings or sawdust on which the finest specimens are almost invariably found. Although an edible species, it has nothing to commend it greatly. 8–12 × 5–11cm. Autumn. Edible.

Collectors may occasionally come across one other member of the family, *Volvariella speciosa*, a rather large, dirty white toadstool with a bag-like volva at the stem base. It grows among compost and on rich soil and is often confused with amanitas.

Pluteus cervinus
Fawn Pluteus

ENTOLOMATACEAE Although this is a large family, it is one that has relatively few common species. Like the Volvariaceae described on the previous page, they are characterised by a pink spore print but unlike them do not have free gills.

Nolanea staurospora. This is a common species of grassy places and woodland clearings. The cap is often slightly sticky, partly striated and dark brown but dries rather paler and smoother. The gills are off-white, becoming pink, while the slender stem, which is slightly paler than the cap, also has faint striations. 5–8 × 3–5cm. Autumn. Inedible.

Leptonia sericella. A small, off-white or pale buff cap which is bell-shaped at first, white gills that later turn pinkish, and a thin whitish stem serve to distinguish this pretty little species which occurs among grass in woods and on poor pastures. There are several other small leptonias, some having bright blue colours, but *L. sericella* is the commonest. 2–5 × 0.5–2cm. Autumn. Inedible.

Entoloma nidorosum. This is a tall, slender fungus, having a slightly sticky cap which is grey-brown when wet but dries to almost white. The gills turn from white to pink on aging while the somewhat wavy stem has a powdery white top. The whole fruit body is pervaded by a rather strong 'chemical' smell that some people find rather unpleasant. 5–13 × 3–8cm. Autumn. Inedible.

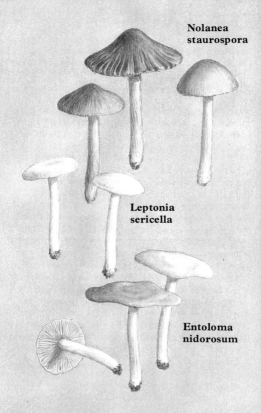

Nolanea staurospora

Leptonia sericella

Entoloma nidorosum

CORTINARIACEAE This is a large and very important family of orange-brown spored fungi, some members of which are highly poisonous. Many of the genera, including *Cortinarius*, the largest and most important of all, have a cobweb-like veil which initially connects the cap to the stem. As the fruit body ages, this tears but remains as a fringe on the cap edge or as delicate bands on the stem. It must be made clear however that this veil is not, as is sometimes imagined, unique to the family.

Cortinarius elatior, C. pseudosalor, C. triumphans. It must be stressed that *Cortinarius* species are extremely numerous and not easy to identify, although few of them are really common. Of the three predominantly brownish species shown here, *C. triumphans* is a birch wood fungus while the other two occur in most types of woodland, but are especially frequent under beech trees. They are quite often considered to be varieties of the same species, *C. pseudosalor* differing essentially from *C. elatior* in sometimes having a violet tint to the gills when young. Although some *Cortinarius* species are edible, the difficulty of identifying them with certainty and the ever-present possibility of confusion with such fungi as the deadly poisonous pine-wood species, *C. speciosissimus*, means that they are better avoided.
C. elatior 10–15 × 5–10cm. Autumn. Edible.
C. pseudosalor 5–10 × 3–12cm. Autumn. Inedible.
C. triumphans 10–15 × 8–12cm. Autumn. Edible.

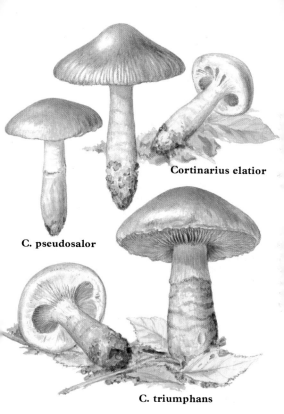

Cortinarius elatior

C. pseudosalor

C. triumphans

**Cortinarius
auroturbinatus**

Cortinarius auroturbinatus. This is a very striking and characteristic *Cortinarius* species of those beech woods lying on chalky soils although there are a number of other, closely related and superficially similar species. The cap, which has an incurved margin, is a shiny, golden-orange colour which later darkens slightly towards the centre. The gills are yellow-brown but these too become olive or rusty coloured later. The stem is yellow with a slightly brownish tinge and the flesh is predominantly white but more yellowish in the swollen, bulbous base to the stem. The whole is pervaded by a sweetish smell. 5–10 × 5–10cm. Autumn. Inedible.

**Cortinarius
anomalus**

C. semisanguineus

Cortinarius anomalus. A common species of mixed and broad-leaved woods with a dull brown or slightly reddish cap, violet gills which soon turn rich brown and a slender, predominantly whitish stem. A number of related and similar species occur also in the same types of woodland.
5–8 × 3–7cm. Autumn. Inedible.

Cortinarius semisanguineus. The commonest of several species that occur in acid birch or coniferous woodland. The most striking feature is the deep blood-red colour of the gills beneath the dull brown cap. The stem is usually paler brown and markedly fibrous. 3–10 × 3–8cm. Autumn. Inedible.

DEADLY POISONOUS

Inocybe patouillardii

Inocybes are fungi to treat with the greatest respect for most of them are poisonous and they should never be eaten. They differ from species of *Cortinarius* in that their gills and spores are darker, cigar-brown and not rusty brown while many species have a slightly woolly or fibrous cap. Although *Inocybe* is a very large genus and many species are quite common, most of them are almost impossible to identify without a microscope.

Inocybe patouillardii, I. geophylla. *I. patouillardii* is a deadly poisonous species; it is sometimes extraordinarily mistaken for the edible field mushroom, but really it is quite different. It is commonest in beech woods on chalky soils but also occurs in other broad-leaved woodland. Although whitish when young, it soon becomes yellower and turns red where the cap cracks. The white gills turn brown later and also become red when damaged. There is a strong fruity smell. *I. geophylla* and its pale lilac form, var, *lilacina* are common fungi of mixed woodland, usually occurring in troops and recognised by the bell-shaped cap and sweet, sickly smell.

I. geophylla 4–9 × 1–3cm. Autumn. **Poisonous.**
I. patouillardii 4–10 × 3–8cm. Summer–Autumn. **Deadly Poisonous.**

Inocybe geophylla

**Inocybe
fastigiata**

Inocybe fastigiata. This and the species shown opposite have a number of features in common. *I. fastigiata* is common in deciduous woodland of all kinds but is most frequent of all in beech woods. It has a dirty, straw yellow coloured, conical to bell shaped cap with pronounced striations, yellowish gills that turn brown and a white or pale ochreous stem, also somewhat striated. Like *I. patouillardii*, this species displays pronounced splitting of the cap edge.

4–10 × 3–10cm. Summer-Autumn. **Very Poisonous.**

Inocybe cookei

Inocybe cookei. A smaller species than *I. fasti-giata* but having some similar characteristics. It occurs in broad-leaved and mixed woodland and has a bell-like or conical cap with a pronounced central bump. The stem is similarly coloured to that of *I. fastigiata* but the gills are more white than yellow-ish although they too darken on aging. Although probably less harmful than some species of *Inocybe*, *I. cookei* is certainly poisonous and, like all the others, should never be eaten.

3–6 × 2–4cm. Autumn. **Poisonous.**

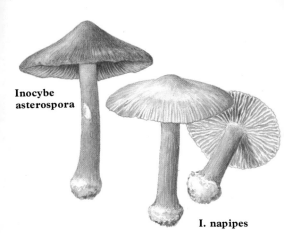

Inocybe asterospora

I. napipes

Inocybe asterospora, I. napipes. Two superficially similar, brown or chestnut coloured *Inocybe* species that differ in a number of respects. *I. asterospora* is a common species in woodland glades or in rich grassland and has a markedly striated cap. The cap of *I. napipes* is much less obviously marked and this species is found in wet birch woods. Both have a bulbous base to the stem but the bulb of *I. asterospora* has a pronounced marginal ridge. Like most *Inocybe* species, both are highly poisonous.
I. asterospora 5–8 × 3–6cm. Autumn. **Poisonous.**
I. napipes. 4–7 × 2–5cm. Autumn. **Poisonous.**

**Crepidotus
mollis**
Soft Slipper
Toadstool

Crepidotus mollis (Soft Slipper Toadstool). A small, gill-bearing bracket fungus, common in groups on logs and stumps of oaks and other broad-leaved trees. It is not at first sight very obviously related to other members of the Cortinariaceae but is placed there by virtue of its spore type and other microscopic features. The cap is yellowish creamy and the gills off-white at first but later turning dark as the yellow-brown spores mature.

Up to 7cm diam. Summer-Autumn. Inedible.

Hebeloma is a small genus of pale brown capped fungi, similar in a number of respects to *Inocybe*, but lacking the fibrous or striated appearance to the cap surface which is usually smooth although it may be slightly sticky.

Hebeloma mesophaeum

Hebeloma mesophaeum. This is a fairly small species with a cap that tends to be darker than that of most members of the genus. The gills are white or almost pinkish while the stem is off-white, tending to become brown towards the base. The taste is slightly bitter and this species is often found on poor damp soils among birch trees although it is characteristic of both deciduous and mixed woodland. Like all hebelomas, it is inedible and may be poisonous. 5–8 × 2–5cm. Autumn. Inedible.

**Hebeloma
crustuliniforme**
Poison Pie

Hebeloma crustuliniforme (Poison Pie). This is probably the most frequently found of all species of *Hebeloma* in Britain. The smooth cap is yellowish-buff with a markedly inrolled margin, pale grey-brown gills and a whitish stem. There is a very pronounced and characteristic smell of radishes, especially when the flesh is broken. *H. crustuliniforme* is to be found growing in rich moist soil in woods and gardens. Sometimes this toadstool is given the English name of Fairy Cake Fungus which is dangerously misleading and Poison Pie much more accurately describes its properties.
4–8 × 5–8cm. Autumn. **Poisonous.**

The genus *Pholiota* includes some very beautiful fungi indeed. Many of the common ones are found on wood, and although some appear to be growing on the ground, in fact most of these arise from buried branches or roots. The stem usually bears a ring and the cap is often scaly.

Pholiota squarrosa. This is probably the most handsome member of the genus and it is also the commonest. The overall appearance is distinctly shaggy. Its cap is a rich ochre colour and patterned with rings of red-brown scales, the gills are deep yellow but later become darkened as the rusty brown spores form, and the ochreous stem has a dark brown ring. It can be found in tufts at the bases of broad-leaved trees and around logs and stumps, especially of beech. Although young specimens are sometimes said to be edible, they are better avoided.
6–18 × 4–10cm. Summer-Autumn. Inedible.

Pholiota flammans. This fungus is similar to, but smaller than the preceding species and is much more yellowish in its overall colouration. In Britain it is a more northerly species and is usually thought of as a Scottish fungus, occuring in small tufts or as solitary individuals on old pine stumps. Indeed, collectors in more southern parts of the country may never see it but sometimes find a number of other members of the genus, especially in broad-leaved woods.
4–12 × 2–6cm. Autumn. Inedible.

**Pholiota
squarrosa**

P. flammans

**Gymnopilus
junonius**

Gymnopilus junonius. *Gymnopilus* differs from
Pholiota mainly in microscopic details of the spores
and they too are very handsome toadstools.
They share the same type of woody habitat however,
G. junonius occurring on the stumps of broad-leaved
trees. It has a deep golden brown cap bearing very
faint scales, whitish or yellowish gills and a pale
yellow-brown stem. There is also a yellowish ring
that often becomes coloured by a deposit of rusty
brown spores. 6–12 × 5–12cm. Autumn. Inedible.

Gymnopilus penetrans

Gymnopilus penetrans. This is a fairly similar species to that described opposite but it occurs on, or very close to the stumps of conifers instead of those of broad-leaved trees. The cap is, again, golden brown but it lacks any proper form of cap scales and the stem lacks a well-formed ring, although a ring-like band of fibrils sometimes betrays where the veil has been. The yellowish gills become increasingly covered with rusty brown spots as they age. 4–7 × 5–8cm. Autumn. Inedible.

Galerina mutabilis

Galerina mutabilis. The genus *Galerina* is closely related to *Pholiota* but the species are smaller and never have scaly caps although some do possess a ring on the stem. *G. mutabilis* is one of those most like a *Pholiota* in its general appearance for it is a rich ochreous brown in colour and bears a pronounced skirt-like ring. It also has similarities to *Pholiota* in its general habit for it is to be found growing in tufts on fallen logs and on stumps of broad-leaved trees. Although it is an edible species, it is not highly recommended.

4–8 × 3–5cm. Spring–Autumn. Edible.

Galerina hypnorum
Moss Pixy Cap

Tubaria furfuracea

Galerina hypnorum (Moss Pixy Cap). *G. hypnorum* is one of the species least obviously related to *Pholiota*. Its pale brown or yellowish toadstools are common among moss in woodland, on lawns or on heaths and it has a characteristic mealy smell and taste which distinguish it from several similar fungi. 2–5 × 0.5–1cm. Spring-Autumn. Inedible.

Tubaria furfuracea. The precise affinities of *Tubaria* are uncertain but the only really common species that collectors need to recognise is *T. furfuracea*, a small, rather dull looking brown-orange fungus found in woods, gardens or on pathsides. The spore print is pale orange, the gills brown-cinnamon and the stem darker but with a white, rather woolly base. 2–5 × 1–4cm. All year. Inedible.

BOLBITIACEAE This is a small family of brown-spored fungi comprising three genera, each with one common species which are shown on this and the opposite page.

**Bolbitius
vitellinus**
Yellow Cow-pat
Toadstool

Bolbitius vitellinus (Yellow Cow-pat Toadstool). Despite its name, this rather unexciting little fungus occurs among grass on rich soil as well as on dung of various kinds. Although yellow and bell-shaped when young, the cap later opens out and fades to off-white but the most characteristic feature of the species is its extremely fragile straw-coloured stem. 6–11 × 2–4cm. Spring–Autumn. Inedible.

**Agrocybe
erebia**

Conocybe tenera

Conocybe tenera. This little fungus grows among grass in woods and on lawns. The orange-brown cap is bell-shaped and striated, the gills cinnamon coloured and the fragile stem ochre brown. 5–8 × 1–3cm. Spring–Autumn. Inedible.

Agrocybe erebia. This species has a loose, off-white, skirt-like ring on a strong, pale brown stem and also a dull brown cap. The cap has a markedly striated margin and bears dark brown gills beneath. It occurs on rich moist soil among leaf litter. 3–5 × 3–6cm. Autumn. Inedible.

PAXILLACEAE A fairly small family with few common British representatives. They are however, distinctive species with a rusty brown spore print and markedly decurrent gills that peel away easily from the flesh. Experts now consider them to be more closely related to the pore-bearing boletes than to other gill fungi. Although sometimes described as edible, these fungi are highly suspect.

Paxillus involutus (Brown Roll-rim). A very common species of birch woodlands on poor soils, unlikely to be mistaken for any other. The cap is solid looking, usually yellow-brown and with a markedly inrolled margin. The gills too are yellow-brown while the rather darker stem is very characteristically and disproportionately short and stout. 5–8 × 5–12cm. Spring-Autumn. Suspicious.

Paxillus atrotomentosus. This is another, superficially similar species with an even shorter and
stouter stem but it differs significantly in that it does
not occur in broad-leaved woods and is frequent on
the stumps or trunk bases of Scots pines. The cap,
which has a slight central depression, is variably
coloured in differing shades of brown and is often to
be found with an olive tint also. The very crowded
gills are yellowish while the black velvety stem is
usually eccentrically attached to the cap.
5–8 × 8–25cm. Autumn. Suspicious.

AGARICACEAE For many mushroom and toadstool enthusiasts, this is the most important family of all as it includes the edible field mushroom as well as the closely related cultivated species. Nonetheless, the genus *Agaricus* to which they belong does also include some poisonous forms and others that can produce uncomfortable symptoms. The spore print is dark chocolate brown, the gills are free and, in most cases, there is a veil and a ring.

Agaricus campestris (Field Mushroom). It is not safe to assume that all mushroom hunters can be certain of identifying *Agaricus campestris* for there are other, related, white species and it is important to check for a combination of characters. The cap, although predominantly white, can become slightly brown and scaly in the centre as it ages; the gills are very closely spaced, pink at first but later dark brown. The stem is white and solid when young, the ring disappears fairly quickly and there is never any trace of yellowing in the flesh (cf.p. 150). *A. campestris* occurs predominantly on grassland, old, well-manured pastures or old lawns and, like several related species, can occur in rings. It is not usually associated with trees.

4–7 × 5–10cm. Autumn. Edible.

**Agaricus
campestris**
Field Mushroom

Agaricus arvensis
Horse Mushroom

Agaricus arvensis (Horse Mushroom). Two more excellent edible white *Agaricus* species are shown here. *A. arvensis* tends to be the largest of the white species and is found most frequently in the vicinity of stables and byres. The cap is similar to that of *A. campestris* but the gills are white at first (when this fungus is most often confused with deadly amanitas), but later pass through grey and brown to become dull chocolate. There is a large spreading ring, white above but sometimes with yellowish scales beneath. 8–13 × 7–15cm. Autumn. Edible.

Agaricus silvicola
Wood Mushroom

Agaricus silvicola (Wood Mushroom). The Wood Mushroom is somewhat similar to the Horse Mushroom, differing most significantly in its woodland habitat (often associated with conifers), in its swollen stem base and in the ring which, although large, is more skirt-like than spreading. Both species have a distinctive smell of aniseed and although *A. silvicola* in particular does turn slightly yellow when handled or on aging, neither fungus displays the instant and characteristically intense yellowing at the stem base shown by *A. xanthodermus* (p.150). 6–8 × 5–8cm. Autumn. Edible.

**Agaricus
xanthodermus**
Yellow-staining
Mushroom

Agaricus xanthodermus (Yellow-staining Mushroom). A mushroom to know well for it is poisonous
and is the only white *Agaricus* that displays a strong
yellow colouration at the extreme base of the stem
when cut. It occurs in woods, gardens and hedgerows. The gills progress from pale pink to a dirty
grey-brown or chocolate, the stem is somewhat
bulbous at the base and the ring is prominent, skirt-
like and white. The smell is peculiar, rather like
that of ink.
6–10 × 5–12cm. Summer-Autumn. **Poisonous.**

**Agaricus
augustus**

Agaricus augustus. A magnificent woodland mushroom. The cap is dull ochreous with pronounced brown scales while the gills are white at first but later become dark brown. The tall stem bears a skirt-like ring and the whole smells markedly of aniseed. Although bruising yellow, the extreme base of the stem does not turn intense yellow when cut; there is only one brown species that does this and it is not one to be eaten. *A. augustus*, however, is a superb edible fungus.

10–20 × 7–20cm. Summer–Autumn. Edible.

Agaricus langei

Agaricus langei. Two more edible brown mushrooms are shown on this and the facing page. *A. langei* is perhaps the most frequently found of them and occurs quite commonly under broadleaved trees. It has a red-brown, scaly cap and gills that change from pink to dark brown as the spores mature. The stem is white or off-white with a pinkish tinge and the base has no swelling. An additional and very distinctive feature is that the flesh turns bloodred when it is cut.

5–10 × 7–10cm. Autumn. Edible.

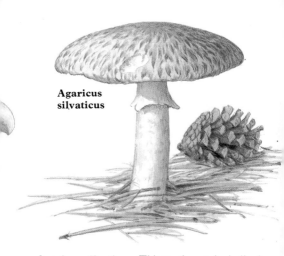

Agaricus silvaticus

Agaricus silvaticus. This mushroom is similar in many respects to *A. langei* shown opposite for it too has a red-brown, scaly cap and gills that also change from pink to dark brown. The stem is similarly coloured too but is generally less stout and has a more or less bulbous base. The flesh differs and turns, at most, pale cinnamon when cut. There are several other brown-capped woodland *Agaricus* species, the slender, slowly reddening *A. variegans* with conifers and the very stout *A. vaporarius*, for example.

5–8 × 6–11cm. Summer-Autumn. Edible.

STROPHARIACEAE This is a family of predominantly brown-spored fungi and includes some remarkably brightly coloured forms, most with a veil and a ring or a marginal fringe to the cap. There are a few edible species but these are uncommon. The family is typified by usually growing on the ground or on stumps.

Stropharia aeruginosa (Verdigris Toadstool). This is a very unusual colour for a fungus; a deep blue green due to the presence of a slimy covering which later tends to dissipate and leave the cap rather yellowish. There is also a bluish green stem and a white ring which often becomes coloured by a showering of spores from the deep brown gills. *S. aeruginosa* is a distinctive species that occurs in a wide range of woodlands, gardens and grassy places.

4–10 × 3–8cm. Spring–Autumn. Suspicious.

Stropharia semiglobata (Dung Roundhead). An unattractive but descriptive name for a very common species that occurs all year round in woods, fields and gardens, usually associated with dung. The markedly rounded cap is ochreous, the gills are dark brown and the stem tall, slender and yellowish with an indistinct little dark brown ring.

5–10 × 1–3cm. All year. Inedible.

**Stropharia
semiglobata**
Dung Roundhead

S. aeruginosa
Verdigris Toadstool

Hypholoma fasciculare (Sulphur Tuft). This is one of the fungi that can usually be recognised from afar, for its lovely sulphur yellow fruit bodies often grow in extremely large clusters around the stumps of broad-leaved trees. Indeed there are few more lovely sights than an autumn morning than to come across a mass of these toadstools adorning a misty woodland. Rather less frequently it can also be found on coniferous wood. The centre of the cap is normally slightly orange while the gills, which at first are green-yellow, later become a dark chocolate brown. The remains of the veil appear as a faint fringe to the cap and also as an indefinite ring-like mark on the stem which is often quite markedly curved and may be proportionately very tall. Although commonest in the autumn, the Sulphur Tuft may be found at most times of the year. The taste is very bitter and although doubtfully poisonous, it is certainly not an edible species. There are a number of other yellowish hypholomas that grow in similar habitats but *H. fasciculare* is the commonest. There are also a few species that occur on boggy or peaty sites but many of these are relatively infrequent (see p.158). 6–12 × 3–7cm. All year. **Poisonous.**

**Hypholoma
fasciculare**
Sulphur Tuft

Hypholoma sublateritium (Brick-red Hypholoma). This attractive toadstool may be thought of as a red version of the Sulphur Tuft shown on the previous page, for it grows in similar habitats (although usually on oak), and also occurs in clusters although these are not usually as large. The individual toadstools however tend to be bigger and have a brick-red cap and stem, the former with some tendency to turn yellowish. The gills moreover are yellow rather than yellow-green and do not darken to the same extent as those of the Sulphur Tuft.

5–10 × 3–8cm. All year. **Poisonous.**

Hypholoma elongatum. There are a number of small, slender hypholomas that are found in woods, on heaths and, especially among moss. *H. elongatum* is typical of them and its honey-yellow caps, at first bell-shaped but later flattening, may be found among damp *Sphagnum*. 4–8 × 1–2cm. Autumn. **İnedible.**

Psilocybe semilanceata (Liberty Cap). This is an infamous little yellow-brown fungus found in troops among grass, by paths and on heathlands. The sharply pointed cap is very distinctive. The gills are cream at first but later darken to almost black, this discolouration affecting the lower part of the cap itself, at first sight giving it the appearance of a *Coprinus*. The species has achieved notoriety as among the harmful effects consequent upon eating it are highly dangerous hallucinations.

4–8 × 1–3cm. Summer-Autumn. **Poisonous.**

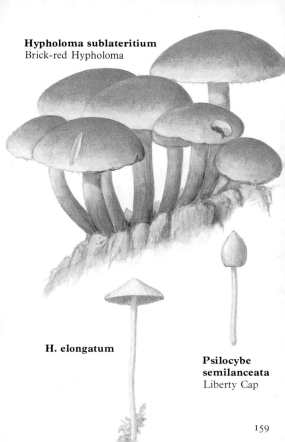

Hypholoma sublateritium
Brick-red Hypholoma

H. elongatum

Psilocybe semilanceata
Liberty Cap

COPRINACEAE This is a family with a number of common, and some very common representatives, the majority in the large genus *Coprinus*. Although some of them are distinctive and readily recognisable fungi, there are many that are confusing, even to experts. The spore print is dark, quite often black and the cap is frequently elongated to the extent of being almost cylindrical.

Psathyrella candolleana (Crumble Tuft), **P. hydrophila.** Psathyrellas are sometimes known descriptively as brittle caps, and the common name Crumble Tuft similarly refers to their extreme fragility. Both of the species shown here are common in tufts on or near the stumps of broad-leaved trees. *P. candolleana* has a creamy white, bell-shaped cap that later flattens and turns whitish. The gills are pale grey-lilac when young but later become dark brown while the remains of the veil usually persist as a fringe around the cap edge. *P. hydrophila* is usually densely tufted. It has a dark brown cap, pale brown but darkening gills and a contrasting whitish stem. It usually bears little trace of the veil although a few fragments may adhere to the cap edge and also as a faint ring-like mark on the stem.
P. candolleana 4–8 × 4–8cm.
Spring–Autumn. Edible.
P. hydrophila 5–10 × 3–6cm. Autumn.
Inedible.

**Psathyrella
candolleana**
Crumble Tuft

P. hydrophila

Panaeolus semiovatus (Egg-shell Toadstool). Species of the genus *Panaeolus* are sometimes called mottle-gills because their black spores mature unevenly over the gill surface, giving it a blotchy appearance. They typically have bell-shaped or ovoid caps and are usually found growing on dung or rich soil. *P. semiovatus* is a particularly large species with a grey-white cap rather like an egg-shell, and a stem with a narrow membranous ring. 5–16 × 2–6cm. Summer-Autumn. Inedible.

**Panaeolus
semiovatus**
Egg-shell
Toadstool

Panaeolus sphinctrinus. P. rickenii. Probably *P. sphinctrinus* is the commonest species of the genus, its greyish stem supporting a grey-black cap with a characteristically 'frayed' margin, like a row of white teeth. *P. rickenii* has, proportionately, the longest stem of the three shown here and is more or less uniformly dark reddish brown although the cap becomes paler as it dries, such that there is often a sharp boundary between the light and dark parts. *P. sphinctrinus* 7–12 × 2–4cm. Summer–Autumn. Inedible. *P. rickenii* 5–10 × 1–2cm. Summer–Autumn. Inedible.

P. sphinctrinus

P. rickenii

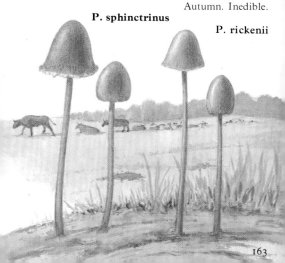

**Panaeolus
foenisecii**

Panaeolus foenisecii. This is a very common little dark brown fungus found on path-sides, pastures and lawns. It has a cap that dries slowly from the tip downwards, giving a characteristically zoned appearance. The gills are eventually dark brown rather than the black of typical *Panaeolus* species, while the slender stem tends to be somewhat paler than the cap. This is certainly an inedible fungus and it has sometimes been thought to be poisonous.
5–8 × 1–3cm. Spring–Autumn. Inedible.

**Lacrymaria
velutina**
Weeping Widow

Lacrymaria velutina (Weeping Widow). *L. velutina* grows among grass; it is closely related to *Panaeolus* but has dark brown spores. The brown-yellow, bell-shaped caps have a somewhat woolly surface and a fringed margin. The gills are dark purple-brown and typically exude little watery drops, so giving the species its common name. The stem is coloured similarly to the cap and is markedly fragile with a dark fibrous ring, below which it is somewhat scaly.
5–12 × 4–8cm. Autumn. Edible.

The genus *Coprinus* is the largest and most important in the family Coprinaceae. Many of the species are small and very difficult to identify but most of the larger forms are quite distinctive. The cap is often cylindrical or bell-shaped and dull-coloured while the gills usually disintegrate to a black inky mass when mature. The spores are more or less black.

Coprinus comatus (Shaggy Ink Cap, Lawyer's Wig). A striking and highly distinctive fungus, unlikely to be mistaken for any other. It occurs in troops or clusters among grass, at roadsides, on rubbish dumps and compost heaps and, rather commonly, among the bare soil of garden beds and fields. It seems particularly to favour ground that has been disturbed and, for this reason, is commonly found on verges after roadworks have been completed. The cap is more or less cylindrical, white with a creamy centre and covered with shaggy white or, more often, pale brownish scales. The stem is white, pinkish or buff with a white ring. The gills are white but later turn pinkish and eventually become a black liquid mass. *C. comatus* is an excellent edible species but it must be collected when young and firm, before the gills have begun to disintegrate. Many people consider it to rank among the most delicious of all toadstools. 10–35 × 3–8cm. Spring–Autumn. Edible.

Coprinus comatus
Shaggy Ink Cap

**Coprinus
atramentarius**
Common Ink Cap

Coprinus atramentarius (Common Ink Cap). A very common species, most usually found in clusters at the base of tree stumps or growing from buried wood in the soil. The cap is grey or brownish grey with prominent striations; the gills are white but later darken to become black; the stem is white and bears a ring-like mark at the base. This is a good edible fungus but, like a number of *Coprinus* species, can cause very unpleasant, although not really dangerous symptoms if eaten with alcoholic drink. 7–15 × 4–8cm. Spring–Autumn. Edible.

Coprinus micaceus (Glistening Ink Cap). This is another species that occurs on stumps or buried wood, often in very large clusters. The fragile and striated cap is rather bell-shaped when young and a rich honey colour sprinkled with glistening particles. The stem is white or off-white.
4–12 × 2–6cm. All year. Inedible.

Coprinus micaceus
Glistening Ink Cap

Coprinus lagopus. The most characteristic feature of this species is the proportionately very long white stem that supports a small woolly, conical, grey-white or buff cap. When older the cap becomes smooth, splits and curls upwards at the margin to reveal the gills which, although white when young, subsequently become black. When this happens, the curled margin appears most attractive – rather like a tiny curled piece of black lace-work. This is usually a solitary species to be found on soil and among leaves in woods and other shady places, although, as with *C. plicatilis*, there are certain similar but less common species that can be found in other types of habitat. 6–12 × 2–5cm. Autumn. Inedible.

Coprinus plicatilis. This attractive little species occurs most frequently as isolated individuals among grass. There are a number of similar, closely related species, some of which occur under hedgerows and in other shady places but they are almost impossible to differentiate without a microscope. *C. plicatilis*, which is sometimes known descriptively as the Japanese Umbrella Toadstool, has a characteristic, strongly grooved, thin buff cap, ovoid at first but later more or less flat. The gills are grey, darkening to black, while the stem is whitish, very slender and fragile. The gills do not liquefy but gradually dry and shrivel. 3–7 × 1–3cm. Spring–Autumn. Inedible.

Coprinus lagopus

C. plicatilis

Coprinus disseminatus, Fairies' Bonnets. This is a very familiar and attractive little species that is almost invariably found in large, sometimes extremely large, troops or clusters on old tree stumps or growing from soil in their vicinity and often intermingled attractively with mosses. It is most unlikely that it will be mistaken for any other toadstool. The tiny cap is buff or almost creamy when young but later it tends to become rather greyish, especially around the margin. It is also slightly downy at first but tends to become smoother as it ages. Initially more or less ovoid, the cap gradually opens to become bell-shaped and is persistently and markedly striated. The stem is fragile, faintly downy and white or greyish. The gills are white when very young but soon turn grey and eventually black but differ from those of most *Coprinus* species in not liquefying.

1–4 × 0.5–1.5cm. Spring–Autumn. Inedible.

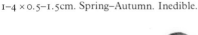

**Coprinus
disseminatus**
Fairies' Bonnets

173

Coprinus cinereus. A typical *Coprinus* in its elongated grey-white cap, white gills that darken to become black before liquefying and a tall, white or buff stem. Distinguishing features are the rather scaly appearance of the cap when young and the swollen stem base that is sometimes extended into a root-like portion below ground. It is one of the commonest and also one of the largest fungi of dung heaps and rotting strawy farmyard debris.

4–12 × 2–5cm. Autumn. Inedible.

**Coprinus
cinereus**

SCHIZOPHYLLACEAE This is a curious little family of fungi that seems to straddle the boundary between the Agaricales and the Aphyllophorales; sometimes they are placed in one group and sometimes in the other. There is only one common European species, and even that is not found very frequently in Britain except in the South-East although it does occur sporadically in other areas.

Schizophyllum commune (Split-gill). This pretty little species has a tiny, bracket-like, grey-white fruit body, often more or less lobed and with a densely hairy upper surface. The margin is markedly inrolled while the pale brown gills characteristically split and curl together when dry, so giving rise to the common name. The fruit bodies occur on fallen timber of broad-leaved trees, often in small groups. Up to 4cm diam. All Year. Inedible

**Schizophyllum
commune**
Split-gill

CANTHARELLACEAE The Aphyllophorales do not produce their spores on gills as most of the Agaricales do, nor inside the enclosed structures formed by the Puff-Balls and their allies. Instead, they produce a wide range of often very beautiful but quite different fruit bodies. The Cantharellaceae are superficially the most similar to the Agaricales, having a crude umbrella shape but with spore-bearing folds on the underside.

Cantharellus cibarius (Chanterelle). The Chanterelle is the commonest of the family and also the most important edible species, being truly exquisite when cooked. It is commonly to be seen dried in continental markets. The cap is more or less funnel-shaped with a wavy rim and the entire fungus is a beautiful egg-yellow, generally slightly paler beneath. It usually occurs in groups under several different types of trees, including beech, oak, birch and conifers. It is often said to be easily confused with the False Chanterelle (p.66) but the latter is really quite different, having true gills, none of the usual apricot scent of *C. cibarius*, a less ragged appearance and is usually a smaller size.

4–7 × 3–11cm. Autumn. Edible.

**Cantharellus
cibarius**
Chanterelle

177

**Cantharellus
infundibuliformis**

Cantharellus infundibuliformis. Although
somewhat similar in general shape to the preceding
species, *C. infundibuliformis* is a much more incon-
spicuous fungus and is easily overlooked among the
leaf litter of the woodland floor as, from above, it can
look very much like a fallen leaf. It is slightly more
slender also and has a fairly dark brown, rather
flabby little cap bearing purple-grey folds beneath
and having a dirty yellow, usually flattened stem. It
too occurs in broad-leaved, mixed and coniferous
woods and although edible, is inferior to the
Chanterelle and is really a rather unappealing little
object. 4–8 × 2–5cm. Summer–Autumn. Edible.

**Craterellus
cornucopioides**
Horn of Plenty

Craterellus cornucopioides (Horn of Plenty).
This rather curious fungus is more extremely
funnel-shaped than either of the two *Cantharellus*
species and has a fairly rough, dark brown interior to
the funnel and a slate grey, spore-bearing surface
tapering down to a black stem. The spore-bearing
surface is also much smoother and often only becomes really wrinkled in old specimens. Commonest
in broad-leaved woods, especially of beech, and
although often well hidden by leaf litter, it is worth
searching for as it is a good species to collect and dry
for the winter and it often occurs in large numbers.
5–12 × 3–8cm. Autumn. Edible.

'CLAVARIOIDS' The fungi illustrated on this plate belong to a group known as the Fairy Club Fungi. They have simple club-shaped fruit bodies and from them a succession of increasingly complex forms can be seen leading through the branched species shown on the next plate to the extraordinary cauliflower-like *Sparassis* shown on p.184. Many species are rare or very rare and only a brief selection of some of the commoner types can be shown here. The classification of all these fungi is still a matter of considerable argument among experts and it is safest for beginners not to try to assign them to specific families.

Clavariadelphus pistillaris. This is the largest of all the Fairy Clubs and it really is a most impressive object. Its dirty yellowish, velvety and dimpled fruit bodies can occasionally be found in broad-leaved woods, especially of beech, and sometimes persist until well into the winter. The whitish flesh has a curious crumbly texture and there is an unpleasant, sickly smell.
Up to 30cm tall. Autumn–Winter. Inedible.

Clavulinopsis fusiformis (Golden Spindles), **C. helvola, Clavaria vermicularis** (White Spindles). These three species are typical of those clavarioids with narrow, spindly fruit bodies. While the orange-yellow *C. helvola* often occurs singly or in small, scattered groups, the golden *C. fusiformis* is formed in small tufted clusters while the brittle, white

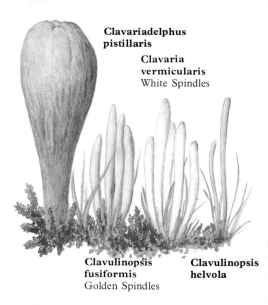

**Clavariadelphus
pistillaris**

**Clavaria
vermicularis**
White Spindles

**Clavulinopsis
fusiformis**
Golden Spindles

**Clavulinopsis
helvola**

C. vermicularis forms dense tufts that are often intermingled with the grass stalks among which it grows.
C. vermicularis and *C. fusiformis* are characteristically species of open grassy places while *C. helvola* is
at least as likely to occur among grass in woodlands
or beneath hedgerows. *C. fusiformis* and *C. vermicularis* both up to 12cm tall. *C. helvola* up to 8cm
tall. All Autumn. Inedible.

Clavulina cristata

Clavulina cinerea, C. cristata. These two species are among the commonest of those whitish clavarioids that have branching fruit bodies usually arising from a single stout stem. Both occur in damp, especially mixed woods and often seem to be particularly abundant along ditches or the sides of small streams. The branches are often somewhat flattened toward the apex, like some antlers, and may end in a fairly sharp point. *C. cinerea* is uniformly grey but *C. cristata* is predominantly white with grey branch tips. *C. cinerea*, *C. cristata* both up to 8cm tall. Autumn. Inedible.

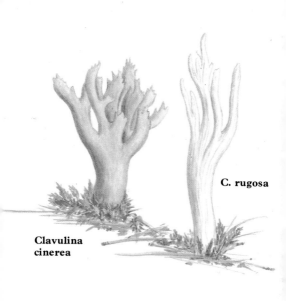

C. rugosa

Clavulina cinerea

Clavulina rugosa. This is yet another pale coloured, branching clavarioid that arises on a single stem. It is, however, one of the tallest of the common species but is much less branched than most of its close relatives and looks at first sight rather like a tall, white Candle-Snuff Fungus (p.234).
Up to 12cm tall. Autumn. Inedible.

Sparassis crispa (Cauliflower Fungus). *Sparassis* is a quite remarkable fungus, more like a slightly ochreous coloured, large, loose-headed and leafless cauliflower than anything, and an object that always arouses interest when it is found for, quite apart from its shape, few British fungi are capable of reaching such a size. It should go without saying that it is unlikely to be mistaken for any other species but, rather unfortunately, it is not very common. It occurs in acid woodland, especially in the close vicinity of pine stumps although similar but smaller forms (possibly separate species), can be found close to oaks. Its curious structure is perhaps best understood if it is thought of as like a giant *Clavulina* (see preceding page) but with flattened and twisted branches and with markedly brittle flesh. It has a rather pleasant, sweetish aroma and, if firm young specimens can be obtained and are well washed to free them of entrapped earth, this fungus can be very good to eat; it may be either baked or fried. A single specimen has been described as 'sufficient for several families'!

Up to 30 × 60cm. Autumn. Edible.

Sparassis crispa
Cauliflower Fungus

HYDNACEAE This interesting family has few common representatives but the one illustrated here (and the two shown on the following plate which are placed in this or closely related groups), are readily identified for the spore-bearing surface on the underside bears a mass of small vertical spines instead of gills, folds or pores. For this reason, some species of the family are commonly known as Hedgehog Fungi.

Hydnum repandum (Wood Hedgehog). This is the most common species of the family and usually occurs in broad-leaved woodland, often in groups or rings, although several related and rare species are confined to northern pine forests. The whitish or buff cap has a flattened or waved, smooth surface with an incurved rim and the stalk is often slightly eccentric, white but somewhat ochreous at the base while the flesh is white and fairly brittle. Although bitter when raw, this species makes excellent eating when cooked. 3–8 × 5–10cm. Autumn. Edible.

Hydnum repandum
Wood Hedgehog

Sarcodon imbricatum

Sarcodon imbricatum. A rare but splendid fungus to be found in coniferous woods on sandy soils, especially in more northern parts and, in Britain, found most frequently in Scottish pine forests. The ground colour of the cap is deep pink but the overlying layer cracks into overlapping red-brown scales. Beneath, there is a mass of brown-purple spines and a short, stout, whitish stem. 5–9 × 6–20cm. Autumn. Edible.

Auriscalpium vulgare (Ear-Pick Fungus). This is a rather pretty little toadstool, related to *Sarcodon imbricatum* by virtue of its tiny brownish spines but otherwise looking very different. The small cap is kidney-shaped and tough and bears a mass of brown-black hairs. The stem too is bristly, swollen at the base and joins the cap in a most unusual and eccentric fashion at one side. The habitat of this fungus is unusual too for it grows on old, buried pine cones from which its cap emerges above the soil on the proportionately very long stem. $1-12 \times 1-2$cm. All Year. Inedible.

Auriscalpium vulgare
Ear-pick Fungus

pine cone
unearthed from
the soil

RESUPINATE FUNGI This group's fruit bodies grow in a curious flattened, skin-like fashion against bark, wood or, less usually, earth. Experts frequently disagree over how these fungi should be classified and here they are treated as a single group.

Phlebia merismoides. A fairly conspicuous, waxy looking fungus forming thick, wrinkled more or less rounded and rather rubbery fruit bodies on dead branches and stumps of broad-leaved trees, especially alders and beech. The colour varies but is most usually predominantly orange. Up to 20cm diam. Autumn-Winter. Inedible.

Merulius tremellosus. Although found in similar habitats to the preceding species, the flattened fruit bodies of this fungus project by up to 4cm at the upper edge to form a distinct, tooth-edged bracket

Phlebia merismoides   **Merulius tremellosus**

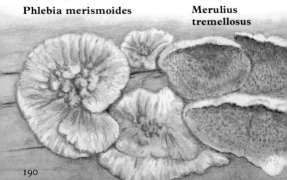

with a white woolly upper surface. Beneath the bracket and over the remaining surface, the colour is an ochre-buff with a marked network of ridges. Up to 15cm diam. Autumn-Winter. Inedible.

Thelephora terrestris. This is a quite extraordinary species that is sometimes very aptly called the earth fan. It is quite commonly found on acid, sandy soils, especially on heathland or under pines where it grows among the needle litter. The fruit body is very tough and fibrous and is dark brown or black above with a paler ragged margin and a slate grey colouration beneath. It is very variable in form and though often more or less horizontal and fan-shaped, several can become closely joined together in a rosette formation which tends to curve upwards at the margins to form a funnel-like structure. Up to 8cm diam. Autumn. Inedible.

**Thelephora
terrestris**

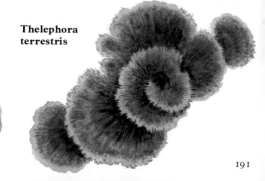

silver-leaf
disease

**Chrondrostereum
purpureum**

Chondrostereum purpureum. Well known to gardeners as the cause of silver-leaf disease of plums and other trees, *C. purpureum* develops either as masses of small, wavy, overlapping brackets or as flattened, crusty plates on dead wood and bark. The brackets may be white, grey or brownish above, more or less woolly and sometimes banded below. Although purple above when young, they later turn brown. Up to 6cm diam. All year. Inedible.

Stereum species are common but not always easy to identify. *S. hirsutum*, below, is not only the most frequently found member of the genus but is also one of the commonest of all fungi. The three species on the next page are also very common.

Stereum hirsutum. Occurs on dead logs, tree stumps and other woody material derived from broad-leaved trees. It forms either brackets or plates with upturned margins, the latter and the undersides of the former being silky smooth and golden, almost egg-yellow. The uppersides of the brackets are hairy and a more dirty yellow. Up to 8cm diam. All Year. Inedible.

▽

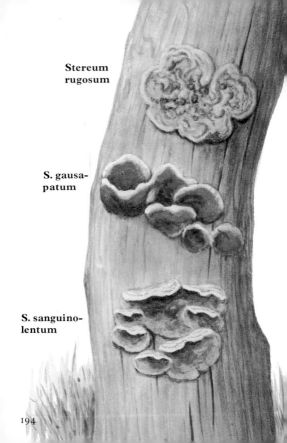

Stereum rugosum

S. gausapatum

S. sanguinolentum

Stereum rugosum, S. gausapatum, S. sanguin-olentum. All three fungi are fairly typical of the genus in their general form although *S. rugosum* tends to adopt the bracket-like form less frequently than the other two and is usually found as a plate or skin-like crust. Its surface is buff-coloured while that of *S. gausapatum* is deep brown and that of *S. sanguinolentum* greyish to almost black. When adopting the bracket type of fruit body, *S. gausapatum* is grey-brown above while *S. sanguinolentum* is grey-white. All three species display an interesting feature, and one that is common to several related types, in 'bleeding' by the exudation of bright red juice when they are scratched or cut – indeed it is this character that gives *S. sanguinolentum* its scientific name. *Stereum rugosum* can be found on fallen branches, stumps and logs of a wide range of broad-leaved trees but seems especially frequent on hazel. Both *S. gausapatum* and *S. sanguinolentum* are important disease-causing agents for they bring about serious decay in living trees; the former being especially important on oaks although occurring on other broad-leaved trees also, and the latter on conifers. *S. rugosum* and *S. gausapatum* up to 5cm diam. *S. sanguinolentum* up to 8cm diam. All three all year. Inedible.

'POLYPORES' Here and on pages 198–211 are illustrated those mostly bracket-shaped members of the Aphyllophorales that bear their spores in pores. Formerly grouped in seven large genera on the basis of gross features of the fruit body, they are now classed in many smaller genera and in a number of families differentiated largely by microscopic features.

Polyporus squamosus (Dryad's Saddle). This is arguably the handsomest European polypore. Although usually forming short-stalked brackets, which can be quite massive, it sometimes produces completely circular fruit bodies like huge, funnel-shaped toadstools. The ground colour above is yellow-ochre but a more or less concentric pattern of dark brown scales is superimposed upon it. Beneath, the pore surface is creamy white.

**Polyporus
squamosus**
Dryad's Saddle

The flesh is fibrous but fairly soft. It is commonest on the trunks of ash and elm trees but occurs on other broad-leaved trees also, usually in small groups. Although edible when young, it is scarcely worth bothering with, being more or less tasteless.

Up to 60cm diam. Spring–Autumn. Edible.

Piptoporus betulinus (Birch Polypore). Anyone strolling into a mature birch woodland in almost any part of Britain except perhaps the more northerly areas will be most unfortunate if they don't find at least some of the trees bearing the very conspicuous fruit bodies of this exceedingly common fungus. Virtually confined to birch trees, *Piptoporus betulinus* is one of the most familiar objects of acid birch woodland. When mature, the almost stalkless bracket is a thick, corky object with a beautiful chalky white pore surface beneath and a grey or very pale brown upper surface which peels off like a skin. This upper surface frequently bears faint and diffuse concentric markings. When younger however, the fruit body is a more or less spherical, white, knob-like object. The Birch Polypore is an important disease-causing agent for it brings about a serious decay of living trees but occurs on fallen branches also and reduces the wood to a reddish crumbly texture. Occurring, as it does, in such quantity, it seems a shame that this is not an edible species. Nonetheless, it has at times proved a useful fungus, strips of the brackets being utilised as razor strops, tinder, as an absorbent or for polishing. In the more northern areas, and especially in Scotland, the place of *P. betulinus* in birch woods is taken by *Fomes fomentarius*, another polypore but one with a very different, hard, hoof-like fruit body.

Up to 20cm diam. Summer–Autumn. Inedible.

Piptoporus betulinus
Birch Polypore

Phellinus igniarius. The massive woody grey-black, white-bordered brackets with grey-brownish undersides occur most commonly on willows although in some parts of Europe they, or related forms, may be found on other broad-leaved trees, especially birches. The upper surface of the bracket is often wrinkled and cracked and formerly they were much used as tinder, being very slow burning.
Up to 25cm diam. All year. Inedible.

Inonotus hispidus. A very distinctive species forming thick brackets with a markedly shaggy upper surface which is rusty brown when young but gradually darkens until almost black. It looks and feels like old damp carpet. The pore surface beneath is yellow, tinged with red and often exudes liquid drops. The brackets are most often seen on ash trees, either singly or in very small groups:
Up to 20cm diam. Autumn. Inedible.

Fistulina hepatica (Beef-steak Fungus). This is an impressive fungus when fresh, forming a bracket like a huge, thick tongue, somewhat rough, gelatinous and deep-reddish above and pinkish beneath with red flesh which exudes a blood-like juice. Most usually seen on oaks in which it causes firstly a wood staining condition known as brown oak and then, finally, decay. The taste is an acquired one, being somewhat acrid and if it must be eaten, it is best collected when young, soaked and then added to stews and cooked for a long time.
Up to 25cm diam. Autumn. Edible.

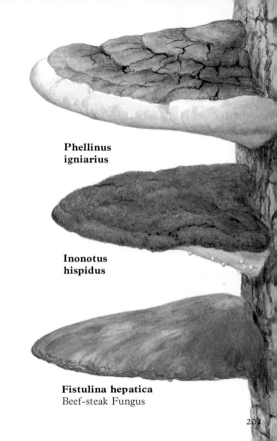

Phellinus igniarius

Inonotus hispidus

Fistulina hepatica
Beef-steak Fungus

Meripilus giganteus. This fungus merits the name 'giganteus' because large clusters of overlapping, fan-shaped brackets invariably occur together. The fruit bodies are sour-smelling, yellowish brown and slightly roughened above with paler, often lobed or wavy margins. Beneath, the pore surface is white but, like the flesh, becomes blackened on handling. It is commonest at the base of broad-leaved trees, especially oak and beech and it is a serious cause of root-rotting of beech trees. Said to be edible but in fact tasteless.

Up to 150cm diam. (en masse).

Autumn–Winter. Edible.

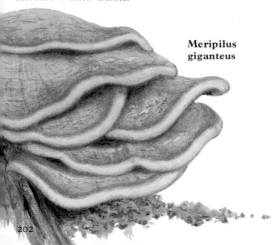

Meripilus giganteus

Grifola frondosa. This species can be thought of as a small version of the preceding one. The fruit bodies are grey-brown above and sprout in large overlapping groups from a common, short stumpy base. They occur at the base of oaks and other broad-leaved trees and, like *M. giganteus*, the pores are white but there is never any blackening. The smell is unpleasant and is said to remind some people of mice. Only the tips of young brackets are worth eating. Occasionally, a small, related species, *G. umbellata*, is found, forming a mass of little branches, each bearing a cap like a miniature umbrella.

Up to 30cm diam. (en masse). Autumn. Edible.

Grifola frondosa

Laetioporus sulphureus

Laetioporus sulphureus. When young this is a beautiful and edible species, producing a mass of overlapping orange brackets from a single stumpy base on stumps or trunks of many types of trees, especially broad-leaved species although it can occur on conifers, particularly yew. The bracket margins and pore surface beneath are vivid sulphur-yellow, sometimes with a reddish tinge, although all parts fade on aging. The surface of the brackets has a kid-glove appearance but the flesh is soft and crumbly like white cheese, producing an aroma that is pleasant to some but sour to others.

Up to 30cm diam. Spring–Autumn. Edible.

**Ganoderma
adspersum**

Ganoderma adspersum. The very distinctive brackets of this fungus occur on most types of broad-leaved trees but are most usually seen on beeches, covering the surrounding vegetation with a deep brown powdery coating of spores. They are shaped like flattened hooves, very hard, wrinkled or lumpy above and with a red-brown colour. The margin is thick and white and the pore surface creamy white but becoming red-brown on handling. There is much confusion between this and a related fungus, *G. applanatum*.
Up to 40cm diam. All year. Inedible.

205

Coriolus versicolor, Bjerkandera adusta.
These two species are very common and are often confused with each other although there are important differences. Both occur on dead wood of broad-leaved trees, producing overlapping masses of thin, tough, rubbery, more or less wavy, concentrically banded brackets with velvety upsides. However, the pore surface of *C.versicolor* is white, that of *B.adusta* greyish; the upper surface of *C.versicolor* is more markedly zoned and generally includes more light brown and yellow than does *B.adusta* while the margin of *C.versicolor* is always persistently white or creamy, whereas that of *B.adusta* darkens with age. *C.versicolor*, up to 5cm diam, *B.adusta*, up to 6cm diam. Both all year. Inedible.

Bjerkandera adusta

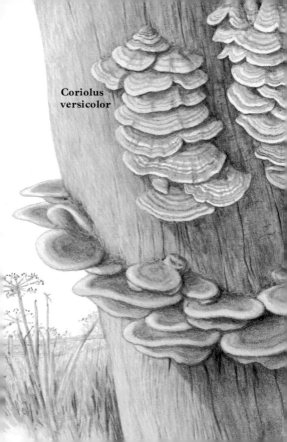
Coriolus
versicolor

Daedalea quercina. This is a very characteristic and common fungus of old, dead oak stumps. The bracket or hoof-like fruit bodies are rather variable in colour but usually tend to be a dirty grey-brown above with concentric bands. When the undersides are examined, the pores will be seen not to be round and small like those of many polypores, but instead are irregular and elongate, forming a pale brown pattern reminiscent of a miniature maze. The flesh, which is pale red-brown, is extremely tough and corky and has a rather pleasant smell.

Up to 15cm diam. All year. Inedible.

Daedalea quercina

**Daedaliopsis
confragosa**
Blushing Bracket

Daedaliopsis confragosa (Blushing Bracket). Another fungus of the dead wood of broad-leaved trees, especially willows. The tough, corky brackets are wrinkled and pale brown above when young but gradually darken to become almost chestnut. The pore surface is white or grey but when bruised, turns characteristically reddish, this being the reason for the common name, Blushing Bracket. The pores, although decidedly elongate, rarely become as labyrinth-like as those of *D. quercina*.
Up to 15cm diam. All year. Inedible.

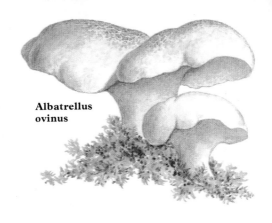

Albatrellus ovinus

Relatively few of the pored fungi in the Aphyllophorales (unlike *Boletus* and its pored allies in the
Agaricales) normally have a mushroom-like form
with a central stalk. Those shown here are among the
best known although they are not closely related to
each other.

Albatrellus ovinus. This rather striking fungus is
a well-known species in many parts of Europe
although it has not yet been found in Britain. It
occurs in damp coniferous woods on rough and
sandy soils and might conceivably exist in such
localities in Scotland. The caps are white when
young but become dirty yellow and misshapen on

aging. The pore surface beneath and the flesh are also white but the latter gradually turns yellow. This fungus makes very good eating and is popular in areas on the Continent where it is common. 3–5 × 10–20cm. Autumn. Edible.

Coltricia perennis. A pretty little fungus, most usually found in small groups on old fire sites in woods or heaths and most unlikely to be mistaken for any other. The cap, which is often markedly funnel-shaped, is red-brown, thin and leathery and has a concentrically ringed, velvety surface above. The pore surface is usually darker brown. 2–8 × 3–8cm. All year. Inedible.

Coltricia perennis

AURICULARIALES/TREMELLALES These two and the next order of fungi are not obviously related to mushrooms and toadstools at all, so different are they in their overall appearance. They are known as the Jelly Fungi because of their characteristic rubbery texture when moist although they are rock-hard when dry. Because of this, their appearance can be misleading and their identification rather difficult if they are found during dry weather.

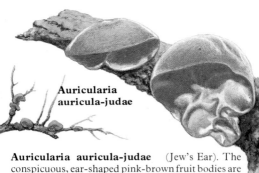

Auricularia auricula-judae

Auricularia auricula-judae   (Jew's Ear). The conspicuous, ear-shaped pink-brown fruit bodies are almost invariable associates of dead elder branches but commonly occur on elms also. They usually occur in groups. Although edible, this species has not achieved in Europe the gastronomic popularity that related forms attain in the Far East where they are commonly cultivated.
Up to 10cm diam. All year. Edible.

Exidia plana (Witches' Butter). These glistening, gelatinous, jet black fruit bodies which grow in
clusters on the dead stumps and logs of broad-leaved
trees (especially oaks) can assume a distorted brain-
like appearance. They are often confused with those
of the quite unrelated and fairly common ascomycete,
Bulgaria inquinans which has an astonishingly similar
general appearance but they can always be distinguished by the minute pimples on the surface.
Up to 5cm diam. All year. Inedible.

Exidia plana

Tremella mesenterica

Tremella mesenterica (Yellow Brain Fungus).
There are around half a dozen species in the genus
Tremella but only two are really common. This
species is similar in general form to *Exidia plana* but
is very much more flimsy and is conspicuously
coloured golden yellow. It occurs in similar habits
but is especially frequent on dead gorse and birch
branches and when fresh and moist, can be spotted
from a considerable distance.
Up to 10cm diam. Autumn–Spring. Inedible.

DACRYMYCETALES. This, the third group of the Jelly Fungi, includes a number of branched and unbranched species that are very like the Clavarioids (p.180) in general appearance but they are readily distinguished by their gelatinous texture. There are many common species but, apart from those illustrated here, few are very easy to identify.

Calocera cornea. This is a rather unimpressive dirty pale yellow fungus found on the dead wood of broad-leaved trees. The highly gelatinous fruit bodies are almost invariably unbranched and occur in clusters, reminiscent of groups of small stubby fingers. Its close relative, *C. viscosa* is much more attractive with slimy, golden yellow, pointed, antler-shaped fruit bodies arising from the roots of coniferous trees.
Up to 3cm tall. All year. Inedible.

Dacrymyces stillatus. There are a number of minute species of jelly fungi in the genus *Dacrymyces* but *D. stillatus* is easily the commonest. The tiny masses of yellow or orange cushion-like fruit bodies are often abundant in wet weather on dead and rotting timber of all kinds and they seem especially frequent on old, wet fence posts.
Up to 0.2cm diam. (en masse). All year. Inedible.

Calocera viscosa

C. cornea

Dacrymyces stillatus

215

PHALLALES In this and the next two orders of Basidiomycetes, the spores are produced either inside a fruit body and are liberated when it bursts, or at the top of a stem which emerges from within the fruit body. The Phallales include some of the most striking, bizarre and, among the tropical species, some of the most beautiful of fungi. There are only two common European forms and they have the additional, unfortunate attribute of a revolting odour.

Phallus impudicus (Stinkhorn). This is an unmistakable species commonly found in woods and gardens and usually detected by its smell of bad drains. The young fruit body is like a jelly-covered egg encased in a whitish skin which emerges above the ground and gives rise to a stout white stem, capped by a slimy dark olive-green mass of spores. The smell attracts flies which remove the spores by feeding on them and, in so doing, reveal a white honeycomb texture beneath. The young egg is edible but is an acquired taste. Up to 25cm tall. Spring–Autumn. Edible.

Mutinus caninus (Dog Stinkhorn). Although basically similar in structure to the preceding species, the Dog Stinkhorn is a smaller fungus with a whitish or yellow-buff stem, and with an orange-red tip beneath the olive-coloured spore mass. The smell, although still unpleasant, is much less pronounced than that of the larger species. Up to 10cm tall. Spring–Autumn. Inedible.

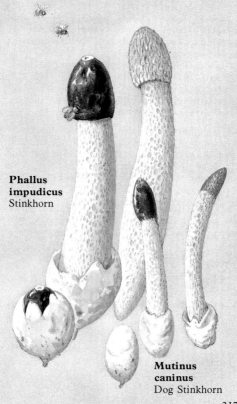

Phallus impudicus
Stinkhorn

Mutinus caninus
Dog Stinkhorn

LYCOPERDALES Like the stinkhorns, the puff-balls too are unmistakable fungi. They have more or less spherical thin-walled fruit bodies with, at maturity, a brown powdery mass of spores within, which is liberated through a small orifice at the top. When they are young however, the flesh is white and firm and at this stage they are edible and delicious, especially sliced thinly and fried.

Lycoperdon pyriforme. This is the only puff-ball to grow on decaying wood, not on the ground and often occurs in large groups. The pear-shaped fruit bodies are off-white or a pale brown and the surface is at first slightly warty but later smooth. 3–10 × 1–3cm. Summer–Autumn. Edible.

Calvatia excipuliformis. Small puff-ball species are not always easy to identify but this is one of the commonest. It is usually found in grassy places on light sandy soils and is pale yellow-brown, more or less pestle shaped and covered with tiny spines and warts. 8–12 × 3–5cm. Autumn. Edible.

**Lycoperdon
pyriforme**

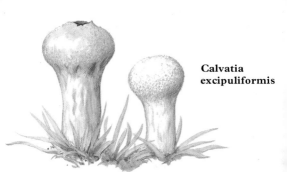

Calvatia excipuliformis

Bovista plumbea. Although whitish when young the skin of this small grassland species later peels back in flakes to expose a thin, grey inner layer. There are several other, related species of *Bovista* of which *B. nigrescens*, with a black inner layer, is the commonest. In windy weather the fruit bodies may become detached and blow around. Up to 3cm diam. Autumn. Edible.

Bovista plumbea

SCLERODERMATALES. This order contains the Earth Balls, a group of fungi that are superficially similar to the Puff Balls shown on the preceding plate but differing in their lack of a single orifice through which the spores are liberated. Instead, the entire fruit body splits up irregularly or simply decays. There is considerable confusion over the number of species, the differences between them and their edibility – while they are eaten in some areas, in others they are regarded as poisonous and are best avoided.

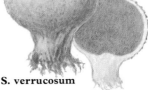

Scleroderma citrinum

S. verrucosum

Scleroderma verrucosum, S. citrinum. Almost certainly the commonest species of Earth Ball is *S. citrinum* which occurs widely in woods, heathland and among short grass. *S. verrucosum* generally grows on richer soil and differs in its larger size, the thinner and slightly rougher fruit body wall, the olive, not dark brown coloured mature spore mass and the obvious root-like structure at the base. Both 4–8cm diam. Autumn–Winter. Inedible.

NIDULARIALES. Possibly the oddest of all common British fungi, the Bird's Nest Fungi are aptly named. The 'eggs' which contain the spores are splashed out of the 'nest' by rain-drops.

Cyathus striatus. Of two fairly frequent *Cyathus* species, *C. striatus* is probably the commonest and can be found on the ground and also occurs on decaying twigs. It has a slightly flaring cup with a fluted inner wall. The related *C. olla* grows quite abundantly on bare soil and differs principally in its smooth wall.

Up to 1cm diam. Spring–Autumn. Inedible.

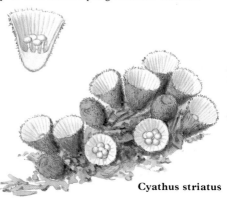

Cyathus striatus

PEZIZALES. The Pezizales constitute one of the most familiar groups of Ascomycetes and are those fungi in which the asci are borne in a more or less open cup or bowl-shaped structure, although in some forms, such as those shown on this and the succeeding two plates, this feature is fairly well disguised as part of a larger fruit body. *Morchella* is the most important genus among a small group of stalked ascomycetes and, although superficially very different, they have similar spores and are classed together on this basis.

Morchella esculenta, M. elata (Morels). As far as true mushroom gourmets are concerned, the Morels are easily the best of the edible spring fungi although unfortunately none of them are very common. *M. esculenta* occurs in broad-leaved woods or in grassland, while the smaller *M. elata* is to be found under conifers or on chalky soils. The hollow white stalk is markedly brittle and has a fine, mealy surface texture. It bears a dark brown to black honeycomb-like head which is elongate in *M. elata* but more spherical in *M. esculenta*. The asci which bear the spores line the shallow pits. Both fungi are very variable, however, and some forms have been described as distinct species. There are many ways in which Morels can be cooked – stewed or fried on their own or used to impart flavour around a joint of meat. *M. esculenta* 8–20 × 3–5cm. Spring. Edible. *M. elata* 5–10 × 1–3cm. Spring. Edible.

**Morchella
esculenta**

M. elata

Gyromitra, *Helvella* and their close relative *Lepto-podia* are common representatives of a stalked group of ascomycetes that are allied to the Morels shown on the preceding page. Like them, they too can display quite wide variations in form. The commonest species of *Gyromitra* and *Leptopodia* are shown on this plate and the two common helvellas on the next. The most obvious feature distinguishing the three is the degree of contortion of the head, ranging from the extreme complexity of *Gyromitra*, through the much less distorted *Helvella*, to the relatively simple *Leptopodia*.

Gyromitra esculenta. This is usually a northern species and can be quite common in its habitat of coniferous woods. The pale brown stem is deeply hollowed and fissured and the variously brown-shaded head, twisted and contorted, like a brain. Despite its name, meaning edible, this is a suspicious species and should be avoided. It is possible that it is only poisonous when fresh, but collectors should not experiment. 7–10 × 12–15cm. Spring. Suspicious.

Leptopodia elastica. This species is obviously related to, but is altogether a more delicate fungus than the broadly similar helvellas shown on the next plate. It has a slender, hollow, more or less smooth white stem and yellow-brown head that, while convoluted, usually seems less ragged than those of its relatives. It occurs in broad-leaved woods and is also definitely suspicious and must not be eaten. 7–10 × 3–5cm. Autumn. Suspicious.

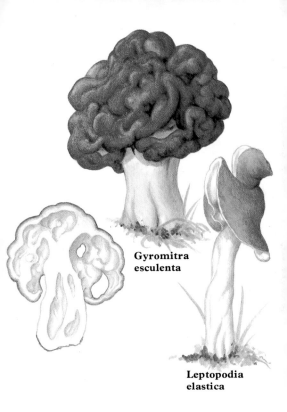

**Gyromitra
esculenta**

**Leptopodia
elastica**

Helvella crispa

Helvella crispa. A distinctive white or creamy-capped fungus to be found in damp places in broad-leaved woods especially along pathsides. It has long, deep furrows on the hollow, pure white stem and a thin, wavy, more or less saddle-shaped, two-lobed head. Like *Gyromitra* and *Leptopodia*, this species is probably best left alone; although some people can eat it with impunity, others suffer ill effects and it should on no account be eaten raw.

8–10 × 4–6cm. Autumn. Suspicious.

**Helvella
lacunosa**

Helvella lacunosa. This is generally similar to the preceding species but has a characteristic, dark grey or almost black upper surface to the lobes of the head which are pale grey and slightly veined beneath. The pale grey stalk is often somewhat swollen at the base and has long deep ridges. Like *H. crispa*, it too occurs in broad-leaved woods and should not be eaten. This is one of a number of species of fungi that quite commonly occur on the burnt ground after old bonfires.

7–10 × 4–6cm. Autumn. Suspicious.

Peziza is a large genus of typically cup-shaped, brownish ascomycetes which are either stalkless or have at best, a very short stalk. The numerous species are fairly readily distinguished from other genera of cup fungi but not easily from each other, even with microscopical examination. All species are either inedible or are not worth bothering with. The three species illustrated here are fairly typical of some of the types that the collector will find but he is equally likely to see others, on sites ranging from the burnt ground beneath old bonfires to the damp floors of cellars.

Peziza badia, P. repanda, P. vesiculosa.

While the stalkless cup of *P. repanda* is usually somewhat wavy, that of the smaller *P. badia* commonly retains a more smooth form until fairly old. The spore-bearing interiors of the cups are pale brown, usually with an olive tint in *P. badia*. The outside of the cups and the broken flesh differ however and the darker red-brown colour of *P. badia* contrasts with the much paler *P. repanda*. Both fungi occur on the ground in woods, *P. repanda* usually growing from richer soils. *P. vesiculosa* is typically found on compost and manure heaps. The cups have a markedly incurved margin and are yellowish brown within and fawn coloured outside. *P. repanda* up to 12cm diam. *P. badia* and *P. vesiculosa* both up to 8cm diam. All Autumn. Inedible.

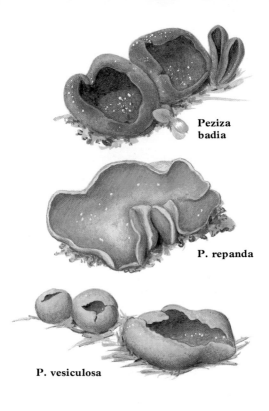

Peziza badia

P. repanda

P. vesiculosa

Cup-shaped ascomycetes, like the pezizas shown on the preceding plate, are very frequently rather dingy in colour. There are however, a number of other, very striking fungi that belong to the same group and which have a distinctive red or orange colouration. The four illustrated here are among the commonest.

Aleuria aurantia

Aleuria aurantia. A truly beautiful fungus, this is found most typically along paths and roadsides but occurs also on bare ground in woods, among gravel and on lawns. It is quite often found with *Lacrymaria velutina* (p. 165). The cups become less regular with age and are a vivid orange within but whitish and downy on the outside. This species is edible but fairly tasteless and is of more value as a table decoration. Up to 10cm diam. Autumn–Winter. Edible.

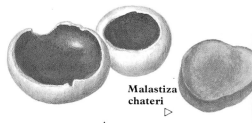

Malastiza chateri

▷

△

Sarcoscypha coccinea. Another very beautiful species, sometimes called the elf-cup. It occurs in groups on dead branches in woods and hedgerows. Up to 4cm diam. Winter. Edible.

Malastiza chateri. A species of damp, bare soil, most often found in extensive clusters. Up to 1.5cm diam. Autumn–Spring. Inedible.

Scutellinia scutellata. This striking species occurs on rotten twigs or on wet ground. The brown outer surface of the cup bears long hairs while the interior is bright red. Up to 1cm diam. Spring–Autumn. Inedible.

Scutellinia scutellata

HELOTIALES 'The Ascomycetes adopt some strange and bizarre forms although as many of them are essentially small fungi, they often go unappreciated. The Helotiales differ from the Pezizales in microscopic features of the spore-bearing ascus. Many have the small familiar cup-like shape but the Geoglossaceae shown on this plate have distinctive, club-like fruiting bodies with the asci and spores on the top or around the sides. The various members of the group are often referred to as earth tongues. There are many different species and several often seem to be found growing together in wet woodland habitats.

Mitrula paludosa

Mitrula paludosa. This species, shown on the opposite page, is a very easily recognised and attractive member of this curious group of fungi, having a yellow-orange club-like head borne on a slender white stalk. It grows on rotten leaves and twigs or among *Sphagnum* moss at stream sides and ditches. Up to 4cm tall. Spring–Summer. Inedible.

Leotia lubrica. This is another distinctive species with a dirty yellow-green, soft and slimy, irregular, button-like cap and a slender, soft and slimy paler stalk. It is found in wet places in broad-leaved woods. Although sometimes given the name Jelly Babies, this should not be taken as an indication that the fungus can be eaten! Up to 6cm tall. Autumn. Inedible.

Leotia lubrica

HYPOCREALES – SPHAERIALES These two groups are typical of those Ascomycetes in which the asci are borne, not in an open cup but in an enclosed flask-like structure, many of which can be grouped together in a relatively massive fruit body. Generally the Hypocreales are bright coloured and the Sphaeriales dark.

Daldinia concentrica. The very common, hard, charcoal-like, rounded blackish fruit bodies of this fungus are most usually seen on ash bark but somewhat smaller forms are found on other broad-leaved trees and are particularly common on birch wood after heath fires. When cut open, concentric rings may be seen within. Up to 4cm diam. All Year. Inedible.

Xylaria hypoxylon (Candle-Snuff Fungus). The ▷ fruit bodies are black at the base and white above with, at first, a simple horn-like shape that later becomes branched like an antler. They usually occur in small clusters on dead and decaying wood of broad-leaved trees. Up to 8cm tall. All Year. Inedible.

Nectria cinnabarina (Coral Spot). This fungus is familiar to gardeners as it not only occurs on dead wood such as old pea sticks but can also cause dying-back of many types of shrub. The dark red fruit bodies containing the ascospores are like minute raspberries but little salmon pink pustules in which different kinds of spore form are more familiar. Up to 0.4cm diam. All Year. Inedible.

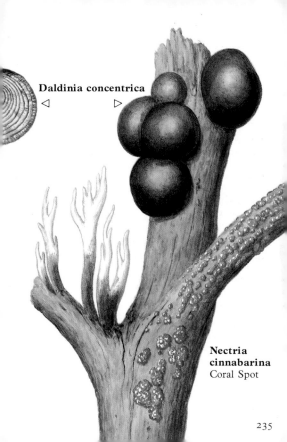

Daldinia concentrica

◁   ▷

Nectria cinnabarina
Coral Spot

235

Index